Modern American Encyclopedia of

Names For Your Baby

Modern American Encyclopedia of

Names For Your Baby

Compiled by the Editors of
American Baby Books

GRAMERCY PUBLISHING COMPANY
New York

This 1986 edition is published by Gramercy Publishing
Company, distributed by Crown Publishers, Inc. by
arrangement with American Baby Books, Inc.

Printed and Bound in the United States of America

Library of Congress Cataloging-in-Publication Data
Main entry under title:
Modern American Encyclopedia of Names For Your Baby

   Reprint. Originally published: Wauwatosa, WI :
American Baby Books, 1981.
   1. Names, Personal—United States.   2. Names,
Personal—English.   3. English language—
Etymology—Names.   I. American Baby Books (Firm)
[CS2377.W53 1986]   929.4'4'0321   85-24922
ISBN 0-517-49011-0
 h g f e d c b a

Contents

A Note Of Introduction

As Shakespeare said so memorably, "A rose by any other name would smell as sweet." But twentieth century psychologists and sociologists present a different view, perhaps best summarized as: "A rose by any other name would *sound less sweet.*"

There is *magic* in a name.

What parents have long suspected has been proven true in formal studies: children with names like Claude and Gladys are perceived less favorably than youngsters with identities more melodically labeled, for example, Melanie or Michael. And in turn, these unfortunately designated children tend to have poorer self-images than their more popularly named counterparts.

Names do count...throughout their bearers' lives and often beyond. Philosophers have said the nature and character of things are condensed and represented in their names. And the act of "naming" is believed to be the earliest of all intellectual accomplishments.

The primary purpose of this book is to provide parents-to-be *inspiration* throughout the process of naming their babies. The names you give your children will be the first gifts you present them...and the most lasting. So the tradition of naming certainly deserves the time and attention you're now granting it.

We'll do our part by offering in these pages all we know about the history and psychology of the name game. You'll learn what names were popular a quarter of a century ago and which are preferred today. You'll also learn which are considered valuable...and which are inexplicably not so highly regarded.

We'll take a look, also, at the ancient—even honored—tradition of bestowing nicknames upon people. Pseudonyms of some famous personalities will be revealed too. (Prepare to be surprised when you discover the actual given names of some of your favorite entertainers!)

The most important information provided within *Modern American Encyclopedia of Names for Your Baby* is, of course, the "dictionary" of girls' and boys' names, their origins and meanings. This is where your creativity is put to the test. Try out your favorites with your surname. Write them down, then speak them aloud. How do they sound together? You —and only you— will know which name is right for the beloved new member of your family.

Use of the dictionary is easy to master. Following each name is its origin and translation as it was literally understood by natives of the originating country. Almost all common Christian names are derived from five languages: Hebrew, Greek, Latin, Celtic, and Teutonic. Hebrew names generally relate to deity; Teutonic names emphasize warlike terms and qualities; Greek, Latin, and Celtic names usually refer to abstract qualities and personal characteristics.

Following each name are a number of its "derivatives": in some cases, they're quite different in sound and spelling. (Ex.: Adelaide—Heidi.) "Curiosities" have been culled and purposefully omitted, for we believe few parents would consider them—and fewer children would enjoy "owning" them.

Choosing a name for a child is one of the most enjoyable decisions a parent will make. So savor these precious moments...and proceed with pleasure.

Congratulations & best wishes,
The Editors

Chapter 1

What's Behind A Name: The History

First or "given" names were used to identify a person long before individuals had both first and last names. They were bestowed upon converts to Christianity at their baptismal ceremonies, so were also designated "christened" names. (The term "Christian" name is a deviation from the correct description, "christened" name.)

Surnames (last names) were regarded as "family names" and came into general use about 1100 A.D. in England, then throughout Europe.

From the first, the church assumed a key role in naming babies, decreeing that only the names of saints and martyrs could be given at baptism. Families derived some comfort from this custom, since they believed their children's hallowed namesakes would protect and support them—a welcome thought as most were struggling to wrest a meager living from the soil.

Even as late as the sixteenth century, the Church of England continued to prohibit the naming of children after "heathen gods." Nothing less than a saint or martyr would do. And since a priest's presence was required at rites of baptism and confirmation, the Church could ensure that its rules were obeyed. Even now, at baptism and in marriage ceremonies, only one name—the christened one—is used.

Original English names were drawn chiefly from the Anglo-Saxon language. Norman names, mostly of Teutonic origin, were bequeathed to us as a direct result of the Norman Conquest of England in 1066.

Twenty years later, William the Conqueror launched a primitive but serious attempt to document "Who's Who" and "Who's Where" in England. His challenging undertaking, referred to as the *Domesday Book* and encompassing all of that country's population, was a pet project because it ascertained his fiscal rights as king. (Owners of vast estates were taxed for their workers as well as their land.) The names recorded show that society then relied almost entirely on a repertoire of 20 names for each sex. About four-fifths of the men were called John, William, Thomas, Richard, Robert, or Henry. The rest were named Roger, Walter, Hugh, Rolf, Edmund, Nicholas, and Philip.

Women were named Agnes, Alice, Cicely, Joan, Matilda, Margaret, Elizabeth, Isabel, Helen, Elaine, Emma, Katharine, Mabel, Sibyl, and Beatrice.

The perennial popularity of these names is obvious from just a brief review of surnames derived from them: John is represented by Jones, Johnson (derived from "son of John"), Johnston, Jenkins, and Jackson. William produced Williams, Williamson, Wilson, Wills, Gill, and Wilkens. Thomas has presented us Thompson, Thomson, Tomkins; and from Richard, we have Richardson, Rickert, and Dickson.

Naturally, the meager supply of first names was reflected in an equally limited choice of surnames. When offspring did not elect to use the customary "son of" or "daughter of" John or William or Thomas, last names were often chosen to reflect the work of the people who lived in the medieval manors and towns, bringing us such common surnames as Smith, Miller, and Cook. Others took their last names from their homeplaces, a custom that afforded us those like Britton (from Britain), Flanders, and Cornwall—plus a multitude of their derivatives.

In the names of men and women today are mirrored the struggles, ambitions, and aspirations of ancient villagers, the habits and work of townspeople, and the daily life of both noble and ignoble.

What's in a name?

Humanity...and nothing less.

Chapter 2

What's In A Name: The Psychology

People generally like—or dislike—certain names as a result of their experiences with persons "labeled" as such. If a fondly remembered childhood pal was known as Sigismunda, it will always seem a melodious title to us. Likewise, if the street corner bully was called Raoul, that name will forever bear negative connotations.

It's also common knowledge that familiar names are more likely to be preferred to those that sound "foreign" to the ear. This inequitable but understandable phenomenon makes it difficult for strangers with unusual names to be taken at face value. Immigrants to this country quickly learned this sad fact. While they could do little about their own names, they "Americanized" the designations of their offspring, often even changing and abridging their surnames. (Fortunately, this custom is steadily changing, now that many people are taking new pride in their ethnic background and naming their children accordingly.)

Research discloses, too, that people generally prefer names that are most popular at the moment. It's not surprising, then, to find statistics that show the majority of people who express dissatisfaction with their names possess those considered "uncommon."

After all, the mere "sound" of a name can have great impact on its owner's life. Ever hear of William Dawes? It's unlikely that you have, yet he rode with Paul Revere to Lexington "that Eighteenth of April, in Seventy-Five," to warn fellow citizens the British were coming. It was Dawes, in fact, who actually made it through enemy lines to accomplish the task of alerting his countrymen; Revere was captured by British soldiers and never reached Lexington.

So why did Longfellow immortalize Revere and ignore Dawes in his celebrated poem, "The Midnight Ride Of Paul Revere"? The name Paul Revere offered more of a "musical lilt" than William Dawes, lending itself better to rhyme!

Even before that, the New World had been named after explorer Amerigo Vespucci, although historians contend he never saw the American continent. An unheralded, obscure mapmaker named Martin Waldseemuller suggested the name America, and so labeled that part of the Western Hemisphere. But for a quirk of fate, patriotic citizens might now be concluding their gatherings with a round of a stirring melody entitled "Waldseemullerland, the Beautiful."

And when Carry Amelia Moore married Mr. Nation, her new name—Carry A. Nation—prompted her to act on her convictions concerning alcohol, for she believed she had been fated to "Carry A Nation" to prohibition. (Aided by the incongruous combination of psalms and hatchets—and like-minded ladies—she did!)

It was no accident, either, that the author Charles Dickens so aptly named the notorious characters from his most beloved books. Scrooge, Blathers, and Bumble were indeed descriptive titles. And wasn't Mr. Micawber every bit as unpleasant as his name suggested?

A name calls forth, in imagery, a portrait of a person. Though it may be implausible, many of us form mental images of people who answer to certain names before we've even met them.

Take Betty, for instance. Upon hearing the name, do you envision Betty Ford, Betty Grable, or Betty Furness? What about the popular name, John? Perhaps you immediately entertain a mental picture of that charismatic president, John Kennedy...or ex-Beatle John Lennon, who met the same tragic fate...or even John Wayne, if you're a "wild western" buff.

There are thousands of Jims, Bobs, Joans, and Janes. And those you've known become part of the mental "association" created each time you hear the name.

"Unreasonable and irrational," you may say.

Unquestionably! But true, nonetheless. And there's little we can do about these preconceived, subconscious notions.

Psychologists, sociologists, and other "students of the mind" have been so intrigued by the phenomenon of name association that they've conducted studies and surveys to determine which names propose "desirable" mental images for most people and which have the opposite effect upon the majority.

A poll conducted by Christopher P. Anderson, author of *The Name Game*, indicates names like Elroy, Claude, Durward, and Gladys are associated with failure, while names such as Keith, Beverly, Douglas, Janet, and Pamela are linked to the concept of success. And in a study conducted by S. Gary Garwood at Tulane University, teachers were found to mark identical essays lower for hypothetical students named Elmer and Bertha than for those signed by Davids and Karens.

The havoc that such bias can wreak upon a child's self-esteem is clear, especially now that studies show young students named Albert, Chester, Mildred, and Phoebe—names rated "undesirable" among teachers polled—score lower in achievement, self-aspiration, and self-concept than children with names judged more desirable.

This phenomenon has even been noted half a world away. Some African tribes habitually name their children after the day of the week upon which they are born, believing the youngsters' personalities can be categorized accordingly. "Wednesday's child," they say, is aggressive and quarrelsome; Monday's is quiet and peace-loving. Is it any wonder, then, that court records from these tribal communities show twice as many "Wednesday children" arrested as those born on Monday? These babies' destinies may very well be predetermined—but by peoples' preconceived notions about them, not by their day of birth!

Again, it's clear there's more in a name than most of us are aware. That's why we end this chapter with a presentation of names generally judged "desirable" and those deemed "undesirable" in recent studies. But before you read them, keep this in mind: Hubert Humphrey did quite well in life. So did Bernard Baruch and Albert Einstein. And who can argue with the accomplishments of Maurice Chevalier, Edith Piaf, and Brigitte Bardot?

In the nebulous area of names, there are exceptions to every "rule." So if you've already fallen in love with one the experts judge "undesirable" and you sincerely believe it will be right for your child, you're well advised to *follow your heart.*

Desirable Names: Girls

Diane	Erin	Jean	Karen
Jennifer	Virginia	Sarah	Linda
Carol	Lisa	Mary	Laura

Desirable Names: Boys

John	Brian	Patrick	Michael
Thomas	Peter	James	Christopher
Jason	Kevin	Robert	Richard

Less Desirable Names: Girls

Bertha	Lucille	Clara	Edith
Hedwig	Mildred	Hilda	Phoebe
Brigitte	Ursula	Emma	Edna

Less Desirable Names: Boys

Elmer	Hubert	Percival	Maurice
Horace	Bernard	Cecil	Reginald
Albert	Hector	Earl	Leon

Chapter 3

Names: The Determining Factors

Now it's down to *business*—the business of naming your child, that is. And inspiration is forthcoming in these popular methods of decision making:

Honoring a relative. If you choose to make your child the "namesake" of a favorite grandparent, aunt, uncle, or other ancestor, you're in good company. About 60 percent of all American babies are named after close relatives. You may want to consider, too, calling your child by his/her mother's maiden name, provided it's suitable and forms a pleasing accompaniment to your surname.

Of course, your fondest desire may be to bequeath your child your name—or that of your spouse. A time-honored tradition it is...and one that will mean much to both of you through the years. But give some thought to what you'll actually call the child to eliminate confusion in your household. A boy named after his father, John, might be dubbed Jack, for instance; a girl named after her mother, Margaret, could be called by the nickname Meg.

If you've titles of two people you wish to honor with your baby's name, why not combine syllables from each and create a name? James and John meld beautifully into Jason; even George and Jean are lovely together as Gena.

Honoring a celebrated person. Many a John Fitzgerald was christened in the 1960s. And Elizabeth is, understandably, a popular name among English children. If you've a hero or heroine whom you admire and his/her name is pleasing when pronounced alongside your surname, you're a step ahead in the naming game. Just be certain the personality you're honoring won't become embarrassingly controversial in the years ahead. (One hopes there weren't too many Benedict Arnolds around in the late 1800s.)

Honoring ethnic heritage. As we mentioned in Chapter Two, Americans previously sought to change names obviously of ethnic origin. But fortunately, this custom is changing now that more and more people are expressing interest and pride in their "roots." The results are some utterly lyrical names for children, as exemplified here:

Greek: Talia, Delia, Dorian.

Hebrew: Leah, Noah, Reuben.

Irish: Kelly, Moira, Sean.

Spanish: Maria, Delores, Miguel.

Scandinavian: Dagmar, Arla, Bjorn.

Turkish: Ali, Halim, Halil.

Honoring an aspiration or ideal. Names such as Faith, Grace, Hope, and Bliss significantly express parents' love for and belief in their children.

Signifying a circumstance of birth. April, May, Tuesday, Noel, Christmas, and Summer are pretty—and self-explanatory—names. Even the child's birthplace can be a source of a distinctive name, as in Madison, Ames, and Dover.

Choosing a "unisex" name. Feminist parents who don't want their children's titles to be blatantly masculine or feminine often prefer "unisex" names like Robin, Lynn, Lindsey, Drew, Leslie, Tony, or Sidney. Each of these titles is distinctive and may, indeed, eliminate the risk of sex bias in some situations. But if this is the course you choose, be aware that your child is likely to receive mail and official documents addressing him/her in the wrong gender and that other such confusion is likely to prevail.

Creating an "anagram." If you've a knack for concocting anagrams—transpositions of the letters of words to make new words—you may want to fashion your child's name from a word that has special significance for you: Capee from "peace," for example.

Now is the time to allow your creativity full rein. In fact, you may feel ready to turn to the dictionary of girls' and boys' names and add to your list of favorites. Once you've collected a few titles that particularly appeal to you, see if they stand up to these "tests":

Will this name still be appropriate when my child is middle-aged? Cissy or Dickie are cute names for babies and young children, but they don't wear well with age. (Some members of African tribes present their babies names at birth, then replace them with new ones when the children reach maturity.)

Is this name difficult to spell or pronounce? One of the principle reasons some Americans legally change their names is to put an end to lengthy explanations regarding the pronunciation and spelling of particularly uncommon ones. Have a heart when it comes to this aspect of the title your child will live with. Hephzibah may appeal to you, but who can spell it . . . much less pronounce it?

Have you inadvertently created a rhyme or "elision" (name that forms a phrase when spoken along with the surname)? No matter how you look at it, it's not fun to go through life with a name like Norman Gorman or Imin Pain. Take every precaution to avoid these pitfalls!

Will you like nicknames derived from this name? Kids love to call each other by pet names, so forego the title of Henry if its common "diminutive," Hank, is anathema to you. If, on the other hand, you're choosing a name because you love its common nickname, why not skip formalities and have the diminutive officially entered on the child's birth certificate? Consider, too, using a contemporary spelling of a nickname. In most cases, that involves ending the name with an "i" in lieu of "y" or "ie"—as in Mari, Toni, and Joni.

Does the name blend euphoniously and rhythmically with your surname? Generally a surname of two or more syllables sounds best with a short given name, while a single-syllable last name requires a longer accompaniment. Examples are Drew Masterson; Christopher Jones. And try not to choose a first name that ends with a vowel if your surname begins with one—Nora Oren is just not melodic.

And A Few Words About Middle Names

Only three of the first presidents of the United States had middle names. It was rare, in fact, for anyone to be graced with more than one given name until about 1750. But now that our population has multiplied many times over and computer technology requires specific identification per individual, it's a rarity for a baby not to be given a middle name at birth. (The army and navy generally proffer the undignified abbreviation "NMI"—no middle initial— when a recruit's parents have failed to present this third title to him/her.)

When selecting your baby's middle name, two simple guidelines can help. First, keep it euphoniously and rhythmically "in tune" with the given and surnames—brief if they are long and vice versa. Examples are Katherine Ann Collingwood; Mark Huntington Smith. Then, take care that the three initials don't form an embarrassing word, such as "HAG" or "SAD." While this may seem a minor point, it can cause a person to shy away from monograms the rest of his/her life.

Finally, a wife who uses her husband's surname as her own may wish to give their child her maiden name as a middle title. These are often beautiful and distinctive complements to a given name as well as thoughtful remembrances of the baby's maternal grandparents.

Chapter 4

Names: 25 Years Ago

A quarter of a century ago, researchers compiled the following list of 100 girls' names and 100 boys' names, ranking them in their order of popularity. While they weren't necessarily the "prettiest" names of their time, they were the most commonly used.

Girls

Rank	*Name*	*Estimated Number*
1.	Mary	3,720,000
2.	Elizabeth	1,788,000
3.	Barbara	1,785,000
4.	Dorothy	1,770,000
5.	Helen	1,725,000
6.	Margaret	1,485,000
7.	Ruth	1,395,000
8.	Virginia	1,365,000
9.	Jean	1,170,000
10.	Frances	1,155,000
11.	Nancy	1,020,000
12.	Patricia	947,000
13.	Jane	945,000

14.	Alice	900,000
15.	Joan	840,000
16.	Betty	830,000
17.	Dolores	825,000
18.	Eleanor	810,000
19.	Anne	795,000
20.	Florence	750,000
21.	Ann	690,000
22.	Rose	660,000
23.	Lillian	655,000
24.	Marie	645,000
25.	Shirley	640,000
26.	Lorraine	585,000
27.	Irene	570,000
28.	Grace	540,000
29.	Marjorie	525,000
30.	Anna	510,000
31.	Josephine	500,000
32.	Louise	495,000

33.	Mildred	465,000
34.	Janet	460,000
35.	Evelyn	450,000
36.	Marion	440,000
37.	Katherine	420,000
38.	Doris	405,000
39.	Lucille	390,000
40.	Ellen	375,000
41.	Lois	370,000
42.	Marilyn	365,000
43.	Martha	362,000
44.	Harriet	360,000
45.	June	345,000
46.	Bernice	344,000
47.	Jeanne	343,000
48.	Charlotte	330,000
49.	Phyllis	328,000
50.	Loretta	315,000
51.	Katharine	305,000

52.	Elaine	300,000
53.	Carol	287,000
54.	Clara	285,000
55.	Edith	284,000
56.	Sarah	270,000
57.	Gertrude	255,000
58.	Sylvia	252,000
59.	Gloria	250,000
60.	Rosemary	249,000
61.	Sally	247,000
62.	Edna	246,000
63.	Pauline	244,000
64.	Julia	243,000
65.	Joyce	240,000
66.	Susan	235,000
67.	Jacqueline	230,000
68.	Esther	227,000
69.	Marian	226,000
70.	Theresa	224,000

71.	Kathryn	216,000
72.	Caroline	210,000
73.	Rita	208,000
74.	Judith	204,000
75.	Priscilla	200,000
76.	Violet	195,000
77.	Beatrice	190,000
78.	Geraldine	185,000
79.	Hazel	184,000
80.	Beverly	180,000
81.	Norma	179,000
82.	Emma	178,000
83.	Gladys	174,000
84.	Adeline	170,000
85.	Stella	168,000
86.	Carolyn	166,000
87.	Agnes	165,000
88.	Catherine	164,000
89.	Elsie	161,000

90.	Laura	160,000
91.	Constance	155,000
92.	Eileen	154,000
93.	Genevieve	150,000
94.	Rosalie	148,000
95.	Emily	147,000
96.	Cecelia	146,000
97.	Joanne	143,000
98.	Carmella	140,000
99.	Vivian	137,000
100.	Lucy	135,000

Boys

Rank	Name	Estimated Number
1.	John	5,837,000
2.	William	5,365,000
3.	Charles	3,023,000
4.	James	2,998,000
5.	George	2,940,000
6.	Robert	2,404,000
7.	Thomas	1,910,000
8.	Henry	1,668,000
9.	Joseph	1,597,000
10.	Edward	1,407,000
11.	Samuel	1,147,000
12.	Frank	1,120,000
13.	Richard	783,000
14.	Harry	724,000
15.	Francis	707,000
16.	Frederick	705,000
17.	Walter	684,000

18.	David	682,000
19.	Arthur	637,000
20.	Albert	607,000
21.	Benjamin	587,000
22.	Alexander	527,000
23.	Daniel	486,000
24.	Louis	463,000
25.	Harold	374,000
26.	Paul	361,000
27.	Fred	359,000
28.	Edwin	352,000
29.	Andrew	342,000
30.	Alfred	339,000
31.	Peter	334,000
32.	Ralph	300,000
33.	Philip	298,000
34.	Herbert	283,000
35.	Stephen	273,000
36.	Jacob	264,000

37.	Carl	258,000
38.	Theodore	244,000
39.	Clarence	243,000
40.	Ernest	242,000
41.	Michael	235,000
42.	Lewis	221,000
43.	Eugene	220,000
44.	Hugh	200,000
45.	Howard	197,000
46.	Isaac	186,000
47.	Nathaniel	180,000
48.	Roy	178,000
49	Raymond	172,000
50.	Edmund	166,000
51.	Donald	165,000
52.	Lawrence	154,000
53.	Earl	149,000
54.	Horace	148,000
55.	Martin	146,000

56.	Jesse	145,000
57.	Oliver	144,000
58.	Oscar	143,000
59.	Augustus	139,000
60.	Edgar	134,000
61.	Anthony	127,000
62.	Patrick	124,000
63.	Jonathan	123,000
64.	Elmer	122,000
65.	Stanley	117,000
66.	Herman	114,000
67.	Franklin	113,500
68.	Abraham	111,000
69.	Leonard	109,000
70.	Nathan	108,000
71.	Norman	107,000
72.	Russell	106,000
73.	Matthew	105,000
74.	Julius	99,000

75.	Nicholas	98,500
76.	Allen	97,000
77.	Chester	96,000
78.	Leo	92,000
79.	Guy	91,500
80.	Kenneth	91,000
81.	Otto	90,500
82.	Josiah	89,000
83.	Bernard	88,000
84.	Claude	87,500
85.	Christopher	87,000
86.	Sidney	86,500
87.	Harvey	86,000
88.	Moses	84,000
89.	Timothy	83,000
90.	Maurice	82,000
91.	Gilbert	80,500
92.	Archibald	78,500
93.	Jeremiah	78,000

94.	Rufus	77,000
95.	Leon	76,500
96.	Joshua	76,000
97.	Max	75,500
98.	Lloyd	75,000
99.	Warren	74,500
100.	Roger	73,500

...And Now

Like other tastes and preferences, names change with the times. Those "in the news" are often favored, especially when their owners are revered by the public. Even entertainers and fictitious characters from literature exert their influence —a la the surge in usage of Rhett as a boy's name and Scarlett for girls after millions of Americans tuned in to the TV broadcast of that epic movie, *Gone With The Wind*. The current popularity of Sabrina, Jennifer, Tabatha, and Jonathan are also believed to have been inspired by characters on recent hit TV series.

The lifespan of trendy names is brief, though, for Americans are fickle and their heroes and heroines are usually replaced at least once per decade. Names more traditional in nature don't encounter the same problem, yet they can succumb to the dreaded dictum "old-fashioned." The Puritans, for instance, were fond of titles such as Patience, Truth, Faith, Hope, Charity, Moses, and Nathaniel— most of which are considered outdated today. But as so often happens with fashions in everything from clothes to furniture to names, the old Puritan favorites of Joshua, Aaron, and Sarah are now very much back in vogue.

In a poll recently conducted among expectant and new mothers, it's been found that—with certain exceptions—they prefer modern names for girls and traditional names for boys. And while we can't hope to account for that phenomenon, here are the "Top 20" names for boys and girls so you may make your own analysis of the trends:

Top 20 Girls' Names

1. Heather	6. Erin	11. Allison	16. Sara
2. Jennifer	7. Mary	12. Amanda	17. Stacey
3. Jessica	8. Kimberly	13. April	18. Carrie
4. Angela	9. Amy	14. Lisa	19. Danielle
5. Melissa	10. Kelly	15. Nicole	20. Emily

Top 20 Boys' Names

1. Christopher	6. Jason	11. Jeffrey	16. Joseph
2. Brian	7. Kevin	12. Timothy	17. David
3. Joshua	8. Benjamin	13. James	18. Richard
4. Scott	9. Michael	14. Justin	19. Ryan
5. Matthew	10. Mark	15. John	20. Robert

Chapter 5

Modern Baby Names From Around The World

Like last year's swimsuit, the world seems somehow to have "shrunk."

This age of electronic communication—and our "takeover" by TV, in particular —have thrust previously remote areas of the earth right into our living rooms. Simultaneously, supersonic transport quickly deposits American travelers anywhere in the world within hours.

So from either television or personal observation, people today know about other people. They know what they do...how they live...and what their names are. Consequently, titles that once might have sounded curious or exotic have melded into the American cultural milieu.

It's fortunate, then, that so many of these ethnic names are significant and lyrically lovely. They also embody centuries of history and tradition and can, therefore, be a source of pride for a child.

A collection of beautiful names from other lands follows—one specifically for girls, another for boys. Choose carefully if this idea appeals to you.

All titles are considered traditional in their originating countries; most are now gaining popularity in the United States. Many of the names will "fit" perfectly with your surname, while others may need some slight revision to achieve a euphonious blend.

It's appropriate that American children bear names from all nations. After all, excluding the American Indians, every citizen of this country is closely descended from another.

Girls

Aimee	Doni	Joby (i)	Lexie
Alana	Edi	Kala (i)	Lotti
Ali	Elli	Kalle (ie)	Mara (i)
Ami	Franci	Kane	Marni
Bel	Gari	Kari	Marva
Bina	Germaine	Karli	Mega
Birgit	Gina	Karma	Michi
Bo	Ginger	Kasi	Miki
Brooke	Greer	Kelsy (i)	Missie
Cam	Halli	Kisa	Mona
Cara	Harper	Kori (y)	Nani
Carly	Heather	Kristin	Neely
Cher	Hillary	Lani	Neva
Dacy	Holly	Lara	Niki
Danett	Ilana	Laure	Nita
Dede	Ivy	Lea	Nori
Dina	Jani	Lenni	Ona (i)
Dodie	Joana	Lian (Lianna)	Patti

Penni	Ruri	Tara	Willow
Pilar	Sabra	Tawnie	Windi (a)
Poni	Sacha (i)	Teri	Yoki
Randi	Sen	Timmi	Yori
Rani	Shani	Tori	Yvette
Rea	Shira	Trella	Zanette
Ren	Suki	Trini (a)	Zita
Reva	Suzu	Valli	Zuri
Rin	Tala	Veda	
Ruana	Tami (my)	Viki	

Boys

Adar	Berk	Colman	Faber
Adel	Birk	Cowan	Fin (n)
Adri	Blaze	Cris	Flint
Alain	Bond (on)	Dagan	Garth
Alek	Bram	Degan	Hale
Ali	Brandeis	Dane	Hanan
Alrik	Brody	Dar	Hari
Archer	Burr	Davin	Hod (d)
Arel	Cam	Deke	Hollis
Ari	Catalin	Dion	Holt
Arley (i)	Caton	Dore (i)	Hurley
Ash	Chad	Doyle	Jacy
Avi	Chaim	Duff	Javier
Balin	Chase	Dade	Jay
Bane	Cham	Dustin	Jed
Beck	Chi	Dylan	Jin
Bem	Chik	Edan	Jari
Berdy	Clay	Erin	Kane

Kass (Cass)	Mikkel	Rud	Timur
Keddy	Morgan	Sani	Tomi
Keegan	Nigan	Sef	Tymon
Keir	Nari	Shanon	Van
Kell (y)	Odin (on)	Shem	Wen
Keri	Pal	Shen	Yancy
Kerry	Pattin	Slade	Yary (i)
Kim	Purdy	Tad	Yves
Kriss	Ranon	Tait	Zeki
Kyle	Rene	Tano	
Lenn	Robi	Tate	
Mato	Roth	Tem	

Chapter 6

How To Use The Dictionary Of Names

You'll find the following two dictionaries easy to use. The first includes titles traditionally deemed girls'; the second is chock-full of boys' names. Note, too, the many entries in each with both masculine and feminine forms. Now it's simple to name a boy after his mother or a girl after her father—choose a variation of the title that reflects the gender of the child.

For "memory insurance," mark or make a list of the names that seem... somehow... magically right. They are listed alphabetically on the left sides of the pages. Beside each is its origin (in parentheses), then its literal meaning in that native language. (Remember: these are definitions of the name—not a child!)

Finally, each name is followed by those derived from it. If you can't immediately find a particular name, look for one that is similar to it and read through its derivatives. The name you seek may be a variation of another.

"Listen" to your imagination as you read and consider each name as it might apply to your little one. Will she be alert...a "seeker" from the moment she's born? Will his smile be as the sun?

Happy reading—and good luck!

Chapter 7

Girls' Names A–Z

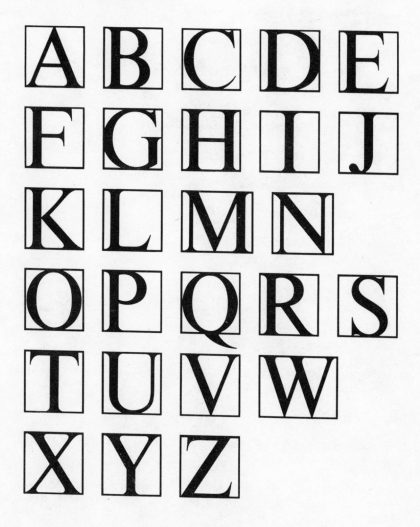

Abigail (Hebrew) "father of joy"; wife of King David. Abbe, Abbey, Abbi, Abbie, Abby, Abigael, Gael, Gale, Gayle, Gail.

Acacia (Greek) "thorny." Cacia, Casey, Casia.

Ada (Teutonic) "prosperous; happy." Short form of Adelaide. Adda, Addie, Adi, Aida.

Adelaide (Teutonic) "noble and of good cheer." Addie, Addy, Adel, Adela, Adele, Adeline, Adelle, Aline, Del, Della, Ellie, Elsie, Elsa, Heidi.

Adeline English form of Adelaide.

Adele French form of Adelaide.

Adina (Hebrew) "delicate." Dena, Dina.

Adora (Latin) "beloved." Dora, Dori, Dorie.

Adrienne (Latin) "dark; rich." Adrea, Adria, Adriana, Adriane.

Agatha (Greek) "the good." Agathe, Aggie, Aggy.

Agnes (Greek) "Pure; gentle; meek." Ag, Aggie, Agna, Agnella, Annis, Ina, Ines, Inez, Nessa, Nessie, Nessy, Una, Ynez.

Aileen (Irish Gaelic) "light." Irish form of Helen. Aila, Ailene, Aleen, Eileen, Eleen, Llene, Lena, Lina.

Aimee French form of Amy.

Alanna (Irish Gaelic) "fair; comely." A feminine form of Alan. Alana, Alaine, Alleen, Allina, Allyn, Lana.

Alberta (Teutonic) "noble and brilliant." A feminine form of Albert. Albertina, Albertine, Ali, Allie, Alverta, Bert, Berta, Bertie, Elberta, Elbertina, Elbertine.

Alcina (Greek) "strong-minded."

Alda (Teutonic) "rich."

Aldora (Greek) "winged gift."

Alexandra (Greek) "helper of mankind." Feminine form of Alexander. Alessandra, Alexa, Alexandrina, Alexina, Alexine, Alexis, Ali, Alix, Allie, Allix, Elena, Lesya, Lexi, Sandra, Sandy, Sondra, Zandra.

Alfreda (Teutonic) "supernaturally wise." Feminine form of Alfred. Alfie, Alfy, Elfreda, Elfrida, Elva, Freda, Freddie, Freida.

Ali Short form of Alexandra or Alice.

Alice (Greek) "truth"; (Teutonic) "noble." Adelice, Aleece, Alicia, Alisa, Alison, Alissa, Allie, Allison, Allyce, Alysia, Alyssa, Elissa, Llysa, Lissa.

Alicia English form of Alice.

Allegra (Latin) "sprightly; cheerful."

Allison (Greek) "little; truthful"; (Teutonic) "famous among the gods." Irish form of Alice. Ali, Alisha, Alison, Alyson, Allie, Alyssia, Lissy.

Alma (Arabic) "learned."

Althea (Greek) "wholesome; healing."

Alvina (Teutonic) "beloved by all." Feminine form of Alvin. Vina, Vinnie, Vinny.

Alvita (Latin) "vivacious, animated."

Alyssa (Greek) "sane, logical."

Amabel (Latin) "lovable." Amabelle, Belle.

Amanda (Latin) "lovable." Manda, Mandy.

Amara (Greek) "of eternal beauty; unfading." Mara.

Amber (Arabic) "amber." As in the semi-precious jewel purported to have curative properties.

Amelia (Latin) "industrious." Amalia, Amelie, Amelina, Ameline, Amy.

Amelinda (Latin) "beloved; pretty." Linda, Melinda.

Amity (Latin) "friendship."

Amy (Latin) "beloved." Aimee, Ame, Ami.

Anastasia (Greek) "of the Resurrection; of springtime." Ana, Anastassia, Stacey, Stacie, Stacy, Tasia.

Andrea (Latin) "womanly." Feminine form of Andrew. Andi, Andreana, Andree, Andria, Andriana, Andy.

Angela (Greek) "the heavenly messenger." Angel, Angelica, Angelina, Angeline, Angelique, Angelita, Angie.

Anita Spanish familiar form of Ann.

Ann, Anne (Hebrew) "graceful; mercy or prayer." An English form of Hannah. Ana, Anette, Anica, Anita, Anna, Annabella, Annabelle, Annetta, Annie, Annis, Anya, Hanna, Hannah, Hanni, Nan, Nana, Nance, Nancy, Nanette, Nanine, Nanni, Nanon, Nettie, Nina, Nita.

Annabel Annabella, Annabelle.

Annette Familiar form of Ann.

Antoinette (Latin) "priceless." A feminine form of Anthony. Antonetta, Antonia, Antonie, Antonietta, Netta, Netti, Nettie, Toni, Tonia, Tonie.

April (Latin) "opening." Aprilette, Avril.

Arabella (Latin) "beautiful altar." Arabelle, Bella, Belle.

Ardelle (Latin) "ardent; zealous." Ardeen, Ardelia, Ardelis, Ardella, Ardene, Ardine.

Ardis (Latin) "fervent or eager"; (Teutonic) "rich gift."

Aretha (Greek) "best."

Aretina (Greek) "virtuous."

Ariel (Hebrew) "lion of God." Ariella, Arielle.

Arlene (Celtic) "pledge." Feminine form of Arlen. Arlana, Arleen, Ariena, Arieta, Arlette.

Arva (Latin) "fertile."

Astra (Greek) "starlike."

Astrid (Teutonic) "impulsive in love."

Atalanta (Greek) "swift huntress." Atlanta.

Atalaya (Spanish-Arabic) "a watch tower."

Athena (Greek) "wisdom."

Auberta (Teutonic) "noble; brilliant."

Audrey (Teutonic) "noble; strong." Audi, Audie, Audra, Audrie, Audry.

Augusta (Latin) "exalted; sublime." Feminine form of Augustus. Augustina, Augustine, Austine, Gussie, Gussy, Tina.

Aurelia (Latin) "golden." Aurelea, Aurora, Ora, Oralee, Orel, Orelee, Orelia.

Aurora (Latin) "dawn." Ora, Rori, Rory.

Ava (Latin) "birdlike."

Avis (Teutonic) "refuge in battle."

Aviva (Hebrew) "springtime." Viva.

Azelin (Hebrew) "spared by Jehovah."

Barbara (Latin) "the stranger." Babette, Babs, Barb, Barbe, Barbee, Barbi, Barbie, Barbra, Barby, Bobbee, Bobbi, Bobby, Bonni, Bonnie, Bonny, Varina.

Bathsheba (Hebrew) "daughter of the oath."

Beatrice (Latin) "she who makes happy." Bea, Beatrix, Bebe, Bee, Trix, Trixie.

Becky (Hebrew) "the ensnarer." Familiar form of Rebecca.

Belinda (Spanish) "beautiful." Name popularized by Alexander Pope (*The Rape of the Lock*). Linda.

Bella (Latin) "beautiful."

Belle (French) "beautiful." Bell, Bella, Billie, Billy.

Benita (Latin) "blessed." Benedetta, Benedicta, Benni, Binnie.

Bernadine (French) "brave warrior." Bernadene, Bernadette, Bernardina, Bernardine, Bernetta, Bernette, Bernie.

Bernice (Greek) "bringer of victory." Bernie, Bunni, Bunnie, Bunny, Veronica.

Bertha (Teutonic) "bright or glorious." Berta, Bertie, Bertina.

Bertina (Teutonic) "shining."

Beth (Hebrew) "house of God." Short form of Elizabeth.

Betsy, Bette, Betty, Bessie Familiar forms of Elizabeth.

Bettina (Hebrew) "consecrated to God."

Beulah (Hebrew) "married." Beulah is a biblical name for Israel.

Beverly (Teutonic) "from the beaver-meadow." Bev, Buffy.

B

Bonita   (Spanish) "pretty."

Bonnie, Bonny   (French-Latin) "sweet; fair."

Brenda   (Teutonic) "fire-brand."

Brenna   (Celtic) "raven; maid."

Brett   (Celtic) "from Britain."

Briana   (Irish Gaelic) "strong." Feminine form of Brian. Brina, Briney.

Bridget   (Celtic) "resolute strength." Biddy, Birgit, Birgitta, Brigid, Brigida, Brigitta, Brigitte, Brita.

Brittany   (Latin) "from England." Britt, Britta.

Brooke   (Teutonic) "from the brook."

Brunhilda   (Teutonic) "armored battle-maid." Brunhilde, Hilda, Hilde.

Bianca   Italian form of Blanche.

Billie   (Teutonic) "strong-willed." Billy.

Blanche   (Teutonic-Latin) "white; fair." Bellanca, Bianca, Blanch, Blinni.

Blanda   (Latin) "affable; flattering."

Blossom   (Modern) "flower-like."

Blythe   (Anglo-Saxon) "joyous."

Calandra   (Greek) "lark." Cal, Calandria, Calli, Callie.

Calantha   (Greek) "beautiful blossom." Calanthe, Callie.

Calida   (Spanish) "ardent."

Calla   (Greek) "beautiful." Call, Callie.

Callista   (Greek) "most beautiful." Calesta, Calista, Calli, Cally.

Calvina   Latin feminine form of Calvin.

Camille   (Latin) "young ceremonial attendant." Cam, Camila, Camilla, Cammie, Millie, Milly.

Candace   (Greek) "glittering; flowing white." Candi, Candice, Candie, Candis, Candy, Kandy.

Candida   (Latin) "pure white." Candi, Candide, Candy.

Cara   (Celtic) "friend"; (Latin) "dear." Carina, Carine, Carrie.

Cari   (Turkish) "flows like water."

Carina   (Latin) "keel." Carin, Carine.

Carisa   (Latin) "artful."

Carita   (Latin) "charitable."

Carla   Teutonic feminine form of Charles.

Carlie   Familiar form of Caroline, Charlotte.

Carlotta   Italian form of Charlotte.

Camel   (Hebrew) "woodland; park." Carmela, Carmelita, Lita.

Carmen (Latin) "song"; (Spanish) "from Mount Carmel." Carma, Carmencita, Carmina, Carmine, Charmaine.

Carol (Latin) "strong; womanly"; (Old French) "song of joy." Carey, Cari, Carleen, Carlen, Carley, Carlin, Carlina, Carlita, Carlotta, Carlyn, Caro, Carole, Carolina, Carolyn, Carri, Carrie, Carroll, Carry, Cary, Caryl, Charla, Charleen, Charlena, Charlene, Charlotta, Charmain, Charmaine, Cheryl, Cherlyn, Karel, Kari, Karla, Karlen, Karleen, Karlotta, Lola, Lolita, Lotta, Lotte, Lottie, Sharleen, Sharlene, Sharline, Sharyl, Sherrie, Sherry, Sheryl.

Caroline (Latin) "little and womanly." Feminine form of Carl; Charles. Carla, Carlen, Carlene, Carley, Carlin, Carline, Carlita, Carlotta, Carly, Carlynn, Carole, Carolin, Carolynn, Carroll, Cary, Charla, Charlena, Charlene, Karla, Karlene.

Carrie Familiar form of Caroline.

Casey (Celtic) "brave."

Cassandra (Greek) "helper of men; disbelieved by men." Cass, Cassi, Cassie, Cassy, Sandi, Sandy.

Catherine (Greek) "pure." An Anglo-Saxon form of Katherine. Caitlin, Caitrin, Caren, Carin, Caron, Caryn, Cass, Cassy, Catlaina, Catarina, Caterina, Catha, Catharina, Catharine, Catherina, Cathi, Cathie, Cathleen, Cathrine, Cathryn, Cathy, Cati, Caye.

Cecilia (Latin) "blind." Cecile, Cecily, Ceil, Celia, Ciel, Cilka, Cissy, Sisile, Sissy.

Celeste (Latin) "heavenly." Cele, Celestine, Celia, Celie, Celina, Celinda.

Chandra (Sanskrit) "moon-like."

Charity (Latin) "benevolent; loving; charitable." Charis, Charita, Cherri, Cherry.

Charlotte (French) "little and womanly." A French form of Carol. Feminine form of Charles. Carla, Carlene, Carline, Carlotta, Carly, Charla, Charlene, Charmain, Cheryl, Cherlyn, Lola, Lolita, Lotta, Lotti, Lottie, Sharlene, Sherrie, Sherry, Sheryl.

Chastity (Latin) "purity."

Cher (French) "beloved." Cherie, Sher, Sherry.

Cheryl Familiar form of Charlotte.

Chiquita (Spanish) "little one."

Chloe (Greek) "blooming."

Christabel (Latin-French) "beautiful Christian." Christabella, Cristabel.

Christine (Greek) "Christian; anointed." Chris, Chrissie, Chrissy, Christen, Christiane, Christie, Christina, Christy, Chrystal, Cris, Crissy, Cristie, Cristin, Cristine, Cristy, Crystal, Kirsten, Kirstin, Kris, Krissie, Kristen, Kristin, Kristina, Tina.

Cicely English form of Cecilia.

Cindy Short form of Cynthia.

Claire French form of Clara.

Clara (Latin) "clear; bright." Chiarra, Clair, Claire, Clare, Claretta, Clari, Clarice, Clarinda, Clarine, Clarissa, Clarita, Klara, Klarrisa.

Clarissa (Latin) "making famous."

Claudia (Latin) "lame." Feminine form of Claude. Claudette, Claudine.

Clementine (Greek) "the merciful." Clemence, Clementina, Clemmie.

Cleo (Greek) "the famous."

Clover   (Anglo-Saxon) "clover blossom."

Colette   (French-Latin) "a necklace." Collette.

Colleen   (Celtic) "girl." Collie, Colline.

Connie   Short form of Constance.

Constance   (Latin) "constancy; firm of purpose." Connie, Constanta, Constantine, Costanza.

Consuelo   (Spanish) "consolation." Consuela.

Cora   (Greek) "maiden." Corella, Corene, Coretta, Corette, Corey, Corie, Corinna, Corinne, Corry.

Coral   (Latin) "coral."

Cordelia   (Welsh) "jewel of the sea." Cordi, Cordie, Cordy, Delia, Della.

Corliss   (Teutonic) "cheerful; good-hearted."

Cornelia   (Latin) "yellow; horn-colored." Feminine form of Cornelius. Cornela, Cornelle, Nell, Nellie.

Courtney   (Teutonic) "from the court."

Crystal   (Greek) "clear as crystal; brilliantly pure."

Cynthia   (Greek) "moon." Cindy.

Cyrene   (Greek) "water nymph."

Dagmar   (Danish) "joy of the Danes."

Daisy   (Anglo-Saxon) "eye of the day; flower."

Dale   (Teutonic) "from the valley."

Dalila   (African) "gentle." Lila.

Dallas   (Celtic) "wise."

Damara   (Greek) "gentle; mild." Mara, Maris.

Damita   (Spanish) "little noble lady."

Dana   (Scandinavian) "from Denmark."

Danielle   (Hebrew) "judged by God." Feminine form of Daniel. Danni, Dannie, Danny, Danya, Daniela, Danila.

Daphne   (Greek) "laurel tree."

Dara   (Hebrew) "compassion."

Darby   (Celtic) "free man"; (Old Norse) "from the deer estate." Darb, Darbie.

Darcie, Darcy   (Celtic) "dark."

Daria   (Greek) "queenly." Feminine form of Darius.

Darlene   (Anglo-Saxon) "tenderly beloved." Darla, Darline, Darrelle, Daryl.

Daron   (Celtic) "great." Feminine form of Darren.

Davina   (Hebrew) "beloved." Feminine form of David. Davida, Veda, Vida, Vita.

Dawn   (Anglo-Saxon) "dawn."

Deborah   (Hebrew) "bee." Deb, Debora, Debra, Debbi, Debbie, Debby.

Deirdre   (Celtic) "complete wanderer." Dee, Didi.

Delia   (Greek) "visible; from Delos." Dehlia, Delinda, Della.

Delilah   (Hebrew) "pining with desire." Delila, Lila.

Demetria   (Greek) "belonging to Demeter (goddess of harvest)."

Dena   (Hebrew) "vindicated"; (Teutonic) "from the valley." Deana, Deane, Deanna, Dina.

Denise   (French) "adherent of Dionysus (god of wine)." Feminine form of Dennis. Denice, Denni, Dennie, Dinny.

Desiree   (French-Latin) "desired."

Devona   (Anglo-Saxon) "the defender."

Diana   (Latin) "divine." Deana, Diane, Dianna, Dianne, Didi, Dyan.

Dinah   (Hebrew) "vindicated." Dina.

Dionne   (Greek) "divine queen." Dion, Dione, Dionis.

Dixie   (French) "ten; tenth."

Dolly   Greek familiar form of Dorothea.

Dolores   (Spanish) "sorrows." Delores, Dolorita, Lola.

Dominique   (Latin) "belonging to God." Feminine form of Dominic. Domini, Dominica.

Donna   (Latin-Italian) "lady." Donella, Donny.

Dora (Greek) "gift." Dodi, Dody, Doralyn, Doralynne, Doreen, Dorena, Dorette, Dori, Dorie, Dory.

Doris (Greek) "of the sea." Dori, Dorice, Dorris.

Dorothy (Greek) "gift of God." Dasha, Dode, Dody, Dolly, Dorothea, Dorothee, Dorthea, Dottie.

Drusilla (Greek) "dewy eyes." Dru, Drusy.

Dulcie (Latin) "sweetness." Delcina, Dulcea, Dulcine.

Eartha   (Teutonic) "of the earth."

Eda   (Anglo-Saxon) "happy; rich."

Edana   (Celtic) "ardent or fiery."

Eden   (Hebrew) "delightful; pleasant." Edin.

Edith   (Teutonic) "rich gift." Eda, Ede, Edi, Edie.

Edna   (Hebrew) "pleasure or delight." Eddi, Eddie.

Edrea   (Teutonic) "prosperous; powerful."

Edwina   (Anglo-Saxon) "valuable friend." Feminine form of Edwin.

Effie   (Greek) "well spoken of."

Eileen   Irish form of Helen.

Eleanor   (Greek) "light." Form of Helen. Ella, Elle, Ellen, Ellie, Lena, Lenore, Nell, Nora.

Elita   (Old French) "chosen." Lita.

Elizabeth   (Hebrew) "oath of God." Belle, Bess, Bessie, Beth, Betsy, Bette, Bettina, Betty, Elisabeth, Elise, Elissa, Eliza, Elsa, Elsie, Elyse, Isabel, Lib, Libbie, Libby, Lisa.

Ella   (Anglo-Saxon) "elfin."

Ellen   English form of Helen.

Eloise   French form of Louise.

Elvira   (Latin) "the fair." Elva, Elvera, Elvina.

Emily (Teutonic-Latin) "industrious." Form of Amelia. Amelia, Ameline, Amy, Em, Emeline, Emilie.

Emma (Teutonic) "ancestress." Ema, Emelina, Emmalyn, Emmi.

Enid (Welsh) "purity."

Erica (Teutonic) "ever-powerful; regal." Feminine form of Eric. Erika, Ricki, Rickie.

Erin (Celtic) "girl from Ireland." Celtic name for Ireland.

Ernestine (Teutonic) "earnest." Feminine form of Ernest. Erna, Ernaline, Ernesta.

Estelle (Latin) "star." Stella.

Esther (Persian) "the planet Venus." Essie, Ettie, Hettie.

Ethel (Teutonic) "noble."

Etta (Teutonic) "little." Familiar form of Henrietta.

Eudora (Greek) "good or delightful gift."

Eugenia (Greek) "well-born." Feminine form of Eugene. Eugenie, Gene, Gena.

Eunice (Greek) "happy victory."

Eustacia (Latin) "fruitful; tranquil."

Evangeline (Greek) "bearer of glad tidings." Eva, Evangelia, Eve.

Eve (Hebrew) "life." Eva, Evelyn, Evie, Evita, Evonne.

Faith (Latin) "faithful." Faye, Fayth.

Fanchon (Teutonic) "free."

Fanny Familiar form of Frances. Fan, Fannie.

Felice (Latin) "happy." Feminine form of Felix. Felicia, Felicidad, Felicity, Felita.

Fernanda (Teutonic) "adventurer." Feminine form of Ferdinand. Fern.

Fiona (Celtic) "fair." Fionna.

Flavia (Latin) "blonde; yellow-haired."

Fleta (Teutonic) "the fleet; swift."

Fleur (French-Latin) "a flower."

Fleurette (French) "little flower."

Flora (Latin) "blooming; prosperous." Flo, Flora, Florie, Florida, Florrie.

Frances (Latin) "free; from France." Feminine form of Francis. Fan, Fancy, Fannie, Fanny, Fran, Francesca, Franci, Francine, Francoise, Frankie, Frannie.

Freda (Teutonic) "peaceful." Short form of Frederica. Frieda.

Frederica (Teutonic) "peaceful ruler." Feminine form of Frederick. Freddie, Fredericka, Frederique, Rickie, Rikki.

Gabrielle (Hebrew) "God is my strength." Feminine form of Gabriel. Gabriella, Gabie.

Gail (English) "gay; lively." Short form of Abigail. Gael, Gale, Gayle, Gayleen.

Genevieve (Celtic) "white wave." Form of Guinevere. Gena, Geneva, Gennie, Gina, Jenny.

Georgeanne Familiar form of Georgia. Georgeanna.

Georgia (Greek) "husbandman." Feminine form of George. George, Georgette, Georgiana, Georgine.

Geraldine (Teutonic) "with a spear." Dina, Gerri, Jeralee, Jere, Jeri, Jerry.

Germaine (French) "German." Germain, Jermaine.

Gertrude (Teutonic) "spear woman." Gert, Gerty, Trudi, Trudy.

Gilberte (Teutonic) "illustrious pledge." Feminine form of Gilbert. Berta, Berti, Berty, Gigi, Gilberta, Gilli, Gilly.

Gilda (Celtic) "servant of God."

Gillian (Latin) "young, downy-haired child." Jill.

Giselle (Teutonic) "pledge; hostage."

Gladys (Celtic) "princess."

Glenna (Irish Gaelic) "from the valley or glen." Feminine form of Glenn. Glenda, Glennis, Glynnis.

Gloria (Latin) "glorious." Gloriana, Glory.

Golda (Teutonic) "gold."

Grace   (Latin) "graceful." Gracie, Gratiana, Grayce.

Greer   Scotch feminine form of Gregor.

Griselda   (Teutonic) "gray-haired heroine." Zelda.

Guinevere   (Celtic) "white lady." Gennie, Gennifer, Genny, Guenevere, Gwen, Gwenore, Jen, Jennifer, Jenny, Winifred, Winnie.

Gwendolyn   (Celtic) "white-browed." Gwen, Gwendolin, Gwennie, Gwenny, Gwyn, Gwynne, Wendi, Wendie, Wendy.

Gwyneth   (Celtic) "blessed." Gwynne, Winnie.

Gypsy   (English) "wanderer; rover."

Hallie   (Greek) "thinking of the sea." Halli, Hally.

Halona   (American Indian) "fortunate."

Hannah   (Hebrew) "graceful." Hana, Hanna, Hanni, Hannie.

Harriet   (Teutonic) "mistress of the home." Feminine form of Harry. Harriette, Hattie.

Hazel   (Teutonic) "hazelnut tree."

Heather   (English) "flowering heather."

Hedda   (Teutonic) "refuge in strife." Heda, Heddie, Hedwig, Hedy.

Helen   (Greek) "light." Eileen, Elaine, Elana, Eleanor, Eleanore, Elena, Elenore, Ella, Elle, Ellen, Ellie, Ellyn, Helena, Helene, Ilene, Ilona, Lana, Lena, Lenore, Leonora, Lora, Nell, Nellie, Nora.

Helga   (Teutonic) "holy."

Henrietta   (Teutonic) "mistress of the household." Feminine form of Henry. Ettie, Hattie, Henrieta, Hettie.

Hermione   (Greek) "of the earth." Erma, Herminia.

Hester   (Greek) "star."

Hilda   (Teutonic) "woman warrior." Hildy.

Hildegarde   (Teutonic) "fortress." Hilda.

Holly   (Old English) "holly tree."

Honora (Latin) "honorable." Honey, Honor, Nora, Norah.

Hope (Old English) "hope."

Hortense (Latin) "gardener."

Ida   (Teutonic) "happy." Idelle.

Ilana   (Hebrew) "big tree."

Imogene   (Latin) "image." Emogene.

Inez   Spanish form of Agnes.

Ingrid   (Teutonic) "hero's daughter." Inga.

Ione   (Greek) "violet-colored stone."

Irene   (Greek) "peace." Rena.

Iris   (Greek) "rainbow."

Irma   (Latin) "noble." Erma.

Isabel   (Hebrew) "consecrated to God." Belita, Belle, Isabelle.

Isadora   (Latin) "gift of Isis."

Isis   (Greek) "moon goddess."

Ivy   (English) "ivy tree."

Jacinta (Greek) "beautiful; comely; hyacinth flower."

Jacqueline (Hebrew) "supplanter." Feminine form of Jacob (through Jacques). Jackelyn, Jackie, Jaclyn.

Jaime (French) "I love."

Jamie Feminine form of James. Jayme.

Jane (Hebrew) "God's gracious gift." Feminine form of John. Gene, Gianina, Giovanna, Jan, Janelle, Janet, Janette, Janice, Janie, Janina, Janine, Janis, Janith, Jayne, Jean, Jeanette, Jeanne, Jenny, Jessie, Jo Ann, Jo-Ann, Joan, Joanna, Joanne, Johanna, Joni, Jonie, Juanita, Shena.

Jasmine (Persian) "jasmine flower."

Jemima (Hebrew) "dove."

Jennifer (Celtic) "white; fair." Form of Guinevere. Gennie, Jen, Jennie, Jenny.

Jessica (Hebrew) "wealthy." Jessalyn, Jessie.

Jill Familiar form of Julia.

Joan (Hebrew) "God's gracious gift." Feminine form of John. Jody, Joni.

Joelle (Hebrew) "the Lord is willing." Feminine form of Joel.

Josephine (Hebrew) "he shall increase." Feminine form of Joseph. Jo, Joline, Josie.

Joy (Latin) "joy."

Joyce (Latin) "joyous."

Judith (Hebrew) "of Judah."

Julia   (Latin) "youthful." Feminine form of Julius. Juliana, Julie, Juliet.

June   (Latin) "June."

Justine   (Latin) "just." Feminine form of Justin.

Kalika (Greek) "rosebud." Kallie.

Kalinda (Sanskrit) "sun."

Kama (Sanskrit) "love." Mythological: the Hindu god of love.

Kara (Greek) "pure."

Karen Danish form of Katherine. Caren, Kari, Karin.

Katherine (Greek) "pure." Caitlin, Caitrin, Caren, Caron, Cass, Cassie, Cassy, Catlaina, Catarina, Catha, Cathe, Catherine, Cathie, Cathleen, Cathlene, Cathrine, Cathryn, Cathy, Catie, Caty, Caye, Karen, Karena, Kari, Karin, Kassi, Kate, Katerina, Katerine, Katey, Katha, Kathie, Kathleen, Kathryn, Kathy, Katie, Katina, Katrinka, Katti, Kay, Kaye, Kit, Kitty.

Keely (Celtic) "beautiful."

Kelly (Gaelic) "warrior woman."

Kelsey (Old Norse) "from the ship-island."

Kerry (Irish Gaelic) "dark; dark-haired."

Kimberly (Teutonic) "from the royal fortress meadow." Kim.

Kristen Scandinavian form of Christine. Krista, Kristel, Kristi, Kristin.

Lainey   Familiar form of Elaine.

Lana   (English) Form of Helen. Lanna, Lanny.

Lane   (Middle English) "from the narrow road." Lanie, Lanni.

Lani   (Hawaiian) "sky."

Lara   (Latin) "famous."

Larissa   (Latin) "cheerful." Lacey, Lissa.

Laura   (Latin) "crown of laurel." Feminine form of Lawrence. Laure, Laureen, Laurel, Lauren, Laurette, Lora, Loreen, Loren, Lorena, Lorene, Loretta, Lorette, Lori, Lorinda, Lorna.

Laverne   (French) "springlike." Laverna, La Verne, Verna.

Lavinia   (Latin) "purified." Vinni.

Leah   (Hebrew) "weary." Lea, Lee, Leigh.

Lee   (Gaelic) "poetic"; (English) "from the pasture." Leeann, Leanna.

Leila   (Arabic) "dark as night." Lela, Lelah, Lelia.

Leona   (Latin) "lion." Feminine form of Leo.

Leontine   (Latin) "lionlike." Leontyne.

Leslie   (Celtic) "from the gray fort."

Letitia   (Latin) "joy."

Lida   (Slavic) "beloved of the people."

Lila   Short form of Dalila. Delilah, Lillian.

Lillian   (Latin) "lily flower." Lila.

Linda   (Spanish) "pretty."

Lindsay, Lindsey   (Teutonic) "from the linden tree island."

Linette   (Celtic) "graceful"; (French) "linnet (bird)."

Lona   (Middle English) "solitary."

Lorelei   (German) "alluring." Lorilee, Lurleen.

Lorraine   (French) "from Lorraine." Laraine, Lori.

Lotus   (Greek) "lotus flower."

Louise   (Teutonic) "famous woman warrior." Feminine form of Louis. Allison, Aloisia, Aloysia, Eloisa, Eloise, Lois, Lola, Lolita, Lou, Lu, Lulu.

Luana   (Old German-Hebrew) "graceful woman warrior."

Lucy   (Latin) "light." Feminine form of Lucius; Luke. Lucia, Luciana, Lucie, Lucille, Lucinda.

Ludmilla   (Old Slavic) "loved by the people."

Luella   (Old English) "elf." Louella, Lulu.

Luna   (Latin) "shining."

Lydia   (Greek) "from Lydia."

Lynette   Familiar form of Linette; Lynn.

Lynn   (Anglo-Saxon) "a cascade, or light pool below a fall." Linn, Lynne.

Mabel   (Latin) "lovable."

Madeline   (Hebrew) "the tower." Lena, Lynn, Madalyn, Madelaine, Madeleine, Madge, Magdalene, Marlene, Maude.

Mahalia   (Hebrew) "affection."

Maida   (Anglo-Saxon) "Maiden."

Mara   Hebrew form of Mary.

Marcella   (Latin) "belonging to Mars." Marcy.

Marcia   (Latin) "warlike." Marcie, Marsha.

Margaret   (Greek) "pearl." Gretchen, Gretel, Madge, Maggie, Margarette, Margarita, Marge, Margie, Margo, Marguerite, Marjorie, Marjory, Meg, Megan, Meghan, Peg, Peggy, Rita.

Marian   Combination of Mary and Ann. Mariam, Marianne, Marion, Maryann.

Marina   (Latin) "maid of the sea."

Martha   (Aramaic) "lady." Marta, Marti, Martie, Martina, Mattie, Pat, Patti, Patty.

Mary   (Hebrew) "bitter." Commemorating the Virgin Mary, now the most frequently bestowed name in all Christian countries. Its true meaning, long since discarded or lost, is "bitter," a Hebrew word with biblical significance. Mame, Mamie, Mara, Maria, Mariae, Marian, Marianne, Marie, Marilee, Marilyn, Marin, Marion, Marlo, Maryann, Marysa, Maura, Maureen, Mavra, Meridel, Mimi, Minnie, Miriam, Mitzi, Moira, Molly, Muriel.

Matilda   (Teutonic) "mighty." Matty, Maude.

Maureen   (Latin) "dark." Irish familiar form of Mary. Maura, Maurene.

Mavis   (Celtic) "thrush."

Maxine   (Latin) "greatest." Feminine form of Max.

May   (Latin) "great"; (Anglo-Saxon) "kinswoman."

Meade   (Greek) "honey wine."

Meara   (Irish Gaelic) "mirth."

Megan   (Anglo-Saxon) "strong or able." Meg, Meghan.

Melanie   (Greek) "dark-clothed."

Melba   (Greek) "soft; slender."

Melina   (Latin) "canary-colored."

Melinda   (Greek) "dark; gentle." Linda, Lindy, Malinda, Mandy.

Melissa   (Greek) "honey bee." Lissa, Milicent, Millie, Missie.

Melody   (Greek) "song." Melodie.

Meredith   (Welsh) "guardian from the sea." Meridith, Merry.

Merle   (Latin) "blackbird."

Mia   (Italian) "mine; my."

Michelle   (Hebrew) "who is like the Lord?" Feminine form of Michael. Micky, Midge.

Mildred   (Anglo-Saxon) "gentle counselor." Millie.

Millicent   (Teutonic) "strength." Mel, Milicent, Milly, Missy.

Mindy   Familiar form of Melinda; Minna.

Minerva   (Greek) "wisdom."

Minnie   Familiar form of Minerva; Wilhelmina.

Mirabel   (Latin) "extraordinary beauty." Mira.

Miranda   (Latin) "admirable." Mira, Myra.

Miriam   Original Hebrew form of Mary. Mimi, Mitzi.

Mona   (Greek) "solitary"; (Irish Gaelic) "noble."

Monica   (Latin) "advisor." Monique.

Morna   (Celtic) "gentle."

Muriel   (Arabic) "myrrh"; (Irish Gaelic) "sea-bright."

Myrtle   (Greek) "a shrub or tree."

Nadine (French-Slavic) "hope." Nadia, Nady.

Nan Familiar form of Ann. Nana, Nancy, Nanette, Nettie.

Naomi (Hebrew) "pleasant."

Natalie (Latin) "Christmas child."

Natasha Russian familiar form of Natalie.

Neala (Celtic) "chieftainess."

Neda (Slovakian) "born on Sunday." Nedi.

Nerissa (Greek) "of the sea."

Nicole (Greek) "victory of the people." Colette, Cosette, Nicki, Nicola, Nikki.

Nina (Hebrew) "grace"; (Spanish) "little girl."

Noel (Latin-French) "Christmas; born of Christmas day."

Nola (Celtic) "noble; famous."

Norma (Latin) "rule; pattern." Noreen.

Nydia (Latin) "from the nest."

Nyssa (Greek) "beginning." Nissa.

Octavia   (Latin) "eighth." Feminine form of Octavius.

Odelia   (Teutonic) "wealthy." Odette, Odilia.

Olga   (Teutonic) "holy." Helga.

Olivia   (Latin) "olive tree."

Opal   (Hindu) "precious stone."

Ophelia   (Greek) "immortality and wisdom."

Oriana   (Latin) "golden."

Oriole   (Latin) "fair-haired."

P

Paige   (Teutonic) "child."

Pamela   (Greek) "all-honey."

Pandora   (Greek) "all-gifted."

Patricia   (Latin) "of the nobility." Feminine form of Patrick. Pat, Patrice, Patsy, Patty, Tricia, Trish.

Paula   (Latin) "little." Feminine form of Paul. Paulette, Pauline, Polly.

Pearl   (Latin) "pearl." Perle.

Penelope   (Greek) "weaver." Penny.

Petrina   (Latin) "rock." Feminine form of Peter. Pier, Perrine.

Petula   (Latin) "seeker."

Philippa   (Greek) "lover of horses." Feminine form of Philip.

Phoebe   (Greek) "shining." Phebe.

Phyllis   (Greek) "green bough." Phillis.

Portia   (Latin) "offering."

Prima   (Latin) "firstborn."

Priscilla   (Latin) "from ancient times."

Prudence   (Latin) "foresight; intelligence."

Quinta   (Latin) "five; fifth child." Feminine form of Quentin.

Rona (Teutonic) "mighty power." Feminine form of Ronald. Rhona.

Rosalie (Irish) Familiar form of Rose. Rosaleen.

Rosalind (Spanish) "beautiful rose." Ros, Rosalinda, Rosalyn, Roz.

Rosamond (Teutonic) "famous protector."

Rachel (Hebrew) "ewe." Rae, Raquel, Shelly.

Ramona (Teutonic) "mighty or wise protectress." Feminine form of Raymond.

Randy Short form of Randall.

Rani (Sanskrit) "queen." Rana.

Rebecca (Hebrew) "the ensnarer." Becky, Reba, Riva.

Regina (Latin) "queen." Regan, Reggi, Reina, Rina.

Rena (Hebrew) "song."

Renata (Latin) "reborn."

Rhea (Greek) "mother of the gods."

Rhoda (Greek) "a rose."

Risa (Latin) "laughter."

Roberta (Teutonic) "shining with fame." Feminine form of Robert. Bobbie, Robbie.

Robin (Teutonic) "robin." Familiar form of Roberta. Robbie, Robina.

Rochelle (French) "from the little rock." Form of Rachel. Shelly.

Rose (Latin) "rose." Rhoda, Rosaleen, Rosa, Rosalie, Rosella, Rosetta, Rosie, Zita.

Rosemary (Latin) "dew of the sea." Rosemarie.

Rowena (Celtic) "white mane." Rena, Ronnie, Ronnie.

Roxane (Persian) "dawn of day." Roxanna, Roxanne.

Ruby (Latin) "ruby."

Ruth (Hebrew) "friend or beauty."

Sabina (Latin) "Sabine woman."

Sabrina (Latin) "legendary English princess."

Sacha (Greek) "helper of mankind."

Salome (Hebrew) "peaceful." Salome.

Samantha (Aramaic) "listener."

Samara (Hebrew) "from ancient city of Samaria."

Sandra (Greek) "helper of mankind." Sandy.

Sapphire (Greek) "sapphire stone; sapphire blue."

Sarah (Hebrew) "princess." Sadie, Sal, Sally, Sara, Sari, Shara, Shari, Sharon, Sheree, Sherri.

Selena (Greek) "moon." Selene.

Selma (Celtic) "fair." Zelma.

Seraphina (Hebrew) "burning; ardent." Serafina, Seraphine.

Serena (Latin) "calm; tranquil." Rena.

Shaina (Hebrew) "beautiful."

Shani (African) "marvelous."

Shannon (Irish Gaelic) "small; wise." Shane.

Sheba (Hebrew) "from the Sheba."

Sheena Irish form of Jane.

Sheila Irish form of Cecilia. Sheela, Sheilah, Shelley.

Shirley (Old English) "from the white meadow." Sherill, Sher, Sherri, Sherrie, Sherry, Shirleen.

Sibyl (Greek) "prophetess." Cybil, Sibby, Sybil.

Simone (Hebrew) "one who hears." Feminine form of Simon. Simonette.

Sophie (Greek) "wisdom." Sofia, Sofie, Sonia, Sonja, Sonny, Sonya, Sophia.

Stella (Latin) "star."

Stephanie (Greek) "garland." Feminine form of Stephen. Stephani, Stesha, Stevana.

Summer (Old English) "summer."

Susan (Hebrew) "lily." Sue, Suki, Susanna, Susannah, Susanne, Susie, Suzanna, Suzanne, Suzie, Suzy.

Sydney (Old French) "from the city of St. Denis."

Sylvia (Latin) "forest maiden." Silvia, Silvie.

Tabitha (Aramaic) "gazelle." Tabbi, Tabby.

Taffy (Old Welsh) "beloved."

Talia (Greek) "blooming."

Tallulah (Choctaw Indian) "leaping water." Tallie.

Tamara (Hebrew) "palm tree." Tammi, Tammy.

Tammy (Hebrew) "perfection."

Tanya (Russian) "fairy queen."

Tara (Irish Gaelic) "tower." Tarah.

Teresa (Greek) "the harvester." Tera, Terese, Teri, Terri, Terry.

Tessa (Greek) "fourth." Tess, Tessie.

Thalia (Greek) "joyful; blooming."

Thea (Greek) "divine."

Thelma (Greek) "nursling."

Theodora (Greek) "divine gift." Teddie, Theda.

Theresa (Greek) "reaper." Tera, Teresa, Terese, Teri, Terri, Terrie, Terry, Tess, Tessy, Therese, Tracy.

Thomasina (Greek) "little twin." Feminine form of Thomas. Tammi, Tammie, Thomasa, Tommie.

Thora (Teutonic) "thunder." Feminine form of Thor. Tyra.

Tiffany (Greek) "appearance of God." Tiff.

Timothea (Greek) "honoring God." Feminine form of Timothy. Tim, Timmi, Timmy.

Titania (Greek) "giant." Tania.

Toby (Hebrew) "God is good." Feminine of form of Tobias. Tobi.

Tracy (Latin) "courageous." Tracey, Tracie.

Trista (Latin) "the sorrowful."

Tuesday (English) "Tuesday."

Udele   (Anglo-Saxon) "rich; prosperous; ruler of all."

Una   (Latin) "one." Irish form of Agnes. Ona, Oona.

Unity   (English) "unity."

Ursula   (Latin) "little bear." Ursa.

Valentina (Latin) "strong; valiant." Val, Valencia, Valentine, Tina.

Valerie (Latin) "strong." Val, Valaree.

Vanessa (Greek) "butterfly." Nessi, Van, Vanni.

Venus (Latin) "Venus (goddess of beauty)."

Vera (Latin) "true"; (Russian) "faith."

Verna (Latin) "springlike."

Veronica (Latin-Greek) "true image." Form of Bernice. Rossi, Ronnie, Vera, Veronika, Veronique, Vonni.

Victoria (Latin) "the victorious." Feminine form of Victor. Vicki, Vicky, Vikki.

Violet (Latin) "violet flower." Lolande, Lolanthe, Vi, Viola, Violette, Yolande.

Virginia (Latin) "virginal; maidenly." Ginger, Ginny, Jinny, Virgie.

Vivian (Latin) "lively." Viv, Vivianne, Vivien.

Wallis   (Teutonic) "from Wales." Feminine form of Wallace.

Wanda   (Teutonic) "wanderer." Wendi, Wendy.

Wesley   (Old English) "from the west meadow."

Whitney   "from the white island."

Wilhelmina   (Teutonic) "resolute guardian." Feminine form of William. Billi, Billie, Min, Minnie, Velma, Vilma, Willa, Willamina, Willie, Wilma, Wilmette.

Wilona   (Old English) "desired."

Winnifred   (Teutonic) "friend of peace." Freddi, Freddie, Oona, Una, Winnie.

Wynne   (Celtic) "fair." Short form of Gwendolyn.

Xanthe   (Greek) "yellow-haired."

Xaviera   (Arabic) "brilliant." Feminine form of Xavier.

Xenia   (Greek) "hospitable." Xena, Zena.

Yolanda   French form of Violet. Yolande.

Yvonne   (Old French) "archer." Feminine form of Ivar. Ives, Yvette.

Zara (Hebrew) "dawn." Form of Sarah. Zarah, Zaria.

Zita Short form of names ending in "sita" or "zita."

Zoe (Greek) "life."

Zola (Italian) "ball of earth."

Zora (Slavic) "aurora."

Zsa Zsa Hungarian form of Susan.

Chapter 8

Boys' Names A–Z

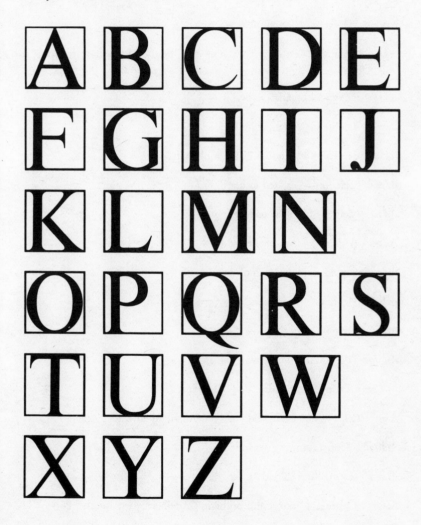

Aaron (Hebrew) "enlightened." Ari, Arnie, Aron, Ron.

Abbott (Hebrew) "father; abbot." Abbie.

Abdul (Arabic) "son of." The name may be used with another name or independently.

Abel (Hebrew) "breath." Abe.

Abner (Hebrew) "father of light."

Abraham (Hebrew) "father of the multitude."

Abram (Hebrew) "exalted father."

Adair (Celtic) "from the oak tree ford."

Adam (Hebrew) "man of the red earth."

Addison (Old English) "son of Adam."

Adlai (Hebrew) "my witness."

Adler (Teutonic) "eagle."

Adolph (Teutonic) "noble wolf." Dolph.

Adrian (Latin) "from Adria, Italy." Adrien, Hadrian.

Alan (Celtic) "handsome; fair." Alain, Allan, Allen, Allie, Allyn.

Alastair Scotch form of Alexander.

Alben (Latin) "fair; blond."

Albert (Teutonic) "noble and brilliant." Adelbert, Al, Albrecht, Bert.

Alden (Old English) "old, wise protector."

Aldous (Old German) "from the old house."

Aldrich (Old English) "old, wise ruler." Aldridge, Eldridge, Rich.

Alexander (Greek) "helper of mankind." Alastair, Al, Alec, Alex, Alexandre, Sandy.

Alfred (Teutonic) "elf counselor." Al, Avery, Fred.

Alger (Anglo-Saxon) "noble spearman." Short form of Algernon.

Algernon (Old French) "bearded."

Ali (Arabic) "greatest."

Allard (Teutonic) "noble; resolute."

Aloysius (Teutonic) "famous in war."

Alphonse (Teutonic) "eager for battle." Alonzo, Alphonso, Fons.

Alvin (Teutonic) "beloved by all."

Ambrose (Greek) "immortal."

Amory (Teutonic) "industrious."

Amos (Hebrew) "burden."

Anatole (Greek) "man from the east."

Andrew (Greek) "manly." Anders, Andre, Andy, Drew.

Angus (Celtic) "exceptionally strong." Ennis, Gus.

Ansel (Teutonic) "divine protector."

Anson (Anglo-Saxon) "son of Ann."

Anthony (Latin) "priceless." Antone, Antonio, Tony.

Apollo (Greek) "manly."

Archer (Latin) "bowman."

Archibald (Teutonic) "bold."

Arden (Latin) "ardent; fervent."

Arlen (Celtic) "pledge."

Armand (Teutonic) "warrior." Armin.

Armstrong (Old English) "strong arm."

Arnold (Teutonic) "mighty as an eagle."

Artemus (Greek) "gift of Artemis."

Arthur (Welsh) "brave."

Arvad (Hebrew) "wanderer."

Arvin (Teutonic) "friend of the people."

Asa (Hebrew) "physician."

Asher (Hebrew) "happy."

Ashley (Teutonic) "from the ash tree meadow."

Aubrey (Teutonic) "ruler of the elves."

August (Latin) "majestic dignity." Historical: the name honors Augustus Caesar. Austin.

Augustine (Latin) "belonging to Augustus." Agustin.

Averill   (Anglo-Saxon) "born in April." Ave, Averil.

Avery   English form of Alfred.

Axel   (Hebrew) "father of peace." Scandinavian form of the Hebrew name Absalom.

B

Bailey   (French) "bailiff; steward."

Baird   (Celtic) "ballad singer." Barr.

Baldwin   (Teutonic) "bold friend."

Bancroft   (Old English) "from the bean field." Ban, Bank, Bink.

Barclay   (Old English) "from the birch tree meadow." Bar, Berk, Berkley.

Barlow   (Old English) "from the bare hill."

Barnabas   (Hebrew) "son of prophecy." Barnaby, Barney.

Barnett   (Teutonic) "bear-like." Barry.

Baron   (Teutonic) "noble warrior."

Bartco   (Old English) "from the barley farm."

Bartholomew   (Hebrew) "son of the ploughman." Bart, Barth, Barthelemy, Bartlett, Bartolome.

Basil   (Greek) "kingly." Basile, Vassily.

Baxter   (Old English) "baker."

Bayard   (Teutonic) "having red-brown hair." Bay.

Beauregard   (Old English) "handsome." Beau, Bo.

Benedict   (Latin) "blessed." Ben, Benedetto, Benito, Benny.

Benjamin   (Hebrew) "son of the right hand." Ben, Benji, Bennie, Jamie.

Benson   (Hebrew) "son of Benjamin."

Benton   (Old English) "of the moors." Bent.

Berkeley Form of Barclay. Berk, Berkly.

Bernard (Teutonic) ''brave bear.'' Barnard, Barney, Bern, Bernardo, Bernhard, Bernie, Berny.

Bert (Teutonic) ''bright.'' Burt.

Bertram (Teutonic) ''glorious raven.'' Bart, Bertrand.

Bevan (Celtic) ''son of Evan.'' Bevin.

Bjorn Scandinavian form of Bern.

Blaine (Celtic) ''thin; lean.'' Blane, Blayne.

Blair (Celtic) ''from the plain.''

Blake (Old English) ''fair-haired and fair-complected.''

Blaze (Latin) ''stammerer.''

Bogart (Old French) ''strong as a bow.'' Bo, Bogie.

Bond (Teutonic) ''tiller of the soil.''

Boone (Old English) ''good.'' Bone, Boonie, Boony.

Booth (Teutonic) ''from the market stall.'' Boothe, Boot.

Borden (Anglo-Saxon) ''from the valley of the boar.''

Boris (Slavic) ''warrior.''

Bowden (Celtic) ''yellow-haired.'' Bowen, Boyd.

Boyce (Teutonic) ''woodland dweller.''

Brad (Old English) ''broad.''

B

Braden   (Old English) "from the wide valley."

Bradford   (Old English) "from the broad river crossing." Brad, Ford.

Bradley   (Old English) "from the broad meadow." Brad, Lee, Leigh.

Bram   (Irish Gaelic) "raven"; (Old English) "fierce; famous."

Brandon   (Teutonic) "from the beacon hill." Bran, Brand, Brandy.

Brendan   (Celtic) "little raven." Bren, Brenden, Brendin, Brendon.

Brent   (Old English) "steep hill."

Bret, Brett   (Celtic) "a Briton, or native of Brittany. Britt.

Brewster   (Old English) "brewer." Brew, Brewer, Bruce.

Brian   (Celtic) "strength; virtue." Briant, Brien, Brion, Bryan, Bryant, Bryon.

Brigham   (Old English) "from the enclosed bridge." Brig.

Brock   (Old English) "badger."

Broderick   (Welsh) "son of Roderick." Brod, Rick, Ricky.

Bronson   (Old English) "son of the dark-skinned one." Bron, Sonny.

Brooks   (Old English) "from the brook."

Bruce   (Old French) "from the brushwood thicket."

Bruno   (Teutonic) "brown-haired."

Bud   (Old English) "messenger." Budd, Buddy.

Burgess   (Teutonic) "citizen of a fortified town." Burr.

Burke   (Teutonic) "from the fortress." Bourke, Burk.

Burl   (Old English) "cupbearer." Burlie.

Burne   (Teutonic) "from the brook." Bourn, Bourne, Burn, Byrne.

Burton   (Teutonic) "from the fortress."

Byrd   (Old English) "birdlike."

Byron   (Teutonic) "from the cottage." Biron.

Calab Von Davis

C

Cadell (Celtic) "with a martial spirit."

Caesar (Latin) "long-haired."

Calder (Celtic) "stream." Cal.

Caldwell (Teutonic) "cold spring." Cal.

✓ *Caleb* (Hebrew) "faithful." Cale.

Calvert (Old English) "herdsman."

Calvin (Latin) "bald." Cal, Vin, Vinnie.

Cameron (Scotch Gaelic) "crooked nose." Cam.

Campbell (Scotch Gaelic) "crooked mouth." Cam, Campy.

Canute (Old Norse) "knot." Knute.

Carey (Old Welsh) "from the fortress." Cary.

Carleton (Old English) "from Carl's farm." Carl, Carlton, Charlton.

Carlin (Celtic) "little champion." Carl, Carlie, Carly.

Carlisle (Old English) "from the walled city." Carlyle.

Carlos Spanish form of Charles.

Carmine (Latin) "song."

Carney (Celtic) "warrior." Car, Carny, Kearney.

Carroll (Celtic) "champion." Familiar form of Charles. Carrol, Cary, Caryl.

Carson (Old English) "son of the family on the marsh."

Carter   (Old English) "cart driver."

Carver   (Old English) "wood carver."

Casey   (Celtic) "brave."

Casper   (Persian) "treasurer." Cass, Gaspar, Gasparo, Jasper.

Cassidy   (Celtic) "clever."

Cassius   (Latin) "vain."

Cato   (Latin) "keen; wise."

Cecil   (Latin) "blind."

Cedric   (Celtic) "chieftain." Rick.

Chad   (Old English) "warlike." Short form of Chadwick, Chadbourne. Familiar form of Charles.

Chaim   (Hebrew) "life." Hy, Hyman, Hymie, Manny.

Chalmers   (Teutonic) "lord of the household."

Chandler   (Old French) "candlemaker."

Channing   (Old English) "knowing"; (Old French) "canon." Chan.

Chapman   (Anglo-Saxon) "merchant." Chappie, Mannie.

Charles   (Teutonic) "manly; strong." Carl, Carlo, Carlos, Carrol, Carroll, Cary, Caryl, Chad, Charley, Charlie, Chick, Chuck, Karl.

Chase   (Old French) "hunter."

Chauncey   (Latin) "chancellor; church official." Chance.

Chen   (Chinese) "great."

Chester   (Old English) "from the fortified town." Short form of Rochester. Ches, Chet.

Chilton   (Old English) "from the farm by the spring."

Christian   (Greek) "follower of Christ." Chris, Christiano, Kit, Krispin, Kris, Kristian.

Christopher   (Greek) "Christ-bearer." Chris, Christoph, Cris, Kit, Kristo.

Clarence   (Latin) "bright; famous." Clare, Clair.

Clark   (Old French) "scholar."

Claude   (Latin) "lame."

Clayborne   (Teutonic) "born of the earth; mortal." Claiborn, Clay, Clayborn, Claybourne.

Clayton   (Old English) "from the town built on the clay bed."

Clement   (Latin) "merciful." Clem, Clemens, Clemente, Klement.

Cleveland   (Old English) "from the cliffs." Cleve.

Clifford   (Old English) "from the cliff at the river crossing." Cliff.

Clifton   (Old English) "steep rock; cliff." Short form of Clifford.

Clinton   (Teutonic) "from the headland farm." Clint.

Clive   (Old English) "cliff dweller."

Clyde   (Welsh) "heard from afar."

Colbert   (Old English) "outstanding seafarer." Cole.

Colby   (Old English) "from the black farm." Cole.

Coleman   (Irish) "dove."

Colin   (Irish Gaelic) "child." Colan, Collin.

Collier   (Old English) "miner."

Conan   (Celtic) "wise." Con, Conant, Connie.

Conlan   (Anglo-Saxon) "hero." Connie.

Conrad   (Teutonic) "able counselor." Con, Connie, Cort, Konrad, Kurt.

Conroy   (Irish) "wise man." Roy.

Constantine   (Latin) "firm; constant." Constantin, Costa.

Conway   (Celtic) "hound of the plain."

Cooper   (Old English) "barrel maker."

Corbin   (Latin) "raven." Corbett, Corby, Cory.

Cordell   (Old French) "ropemaker." Cord, Cordie, Cory.

Corey   (Irish Gaelic) "from the round hill." Cory.

Cornelius   (Latin) "war horn." Connie, Cornell, Nell.

Cosmo   (Greek) "well-ordered." Cos.

Courtland   (Anglo-French) "from the farmstead or court land." Court.

Craig   (Scotch) "from near the crag."

Crandall   (Old English) "from the cranes' valley." Crandell.

Crawford (Old English) "from the ford of the crow." Ford.

Creighton (Old English) "from the town near the creek." Crichton.

Crosby (Teutonic) "from the shrine of the cross." Cross.

Cullen (Celtic) "handsome." Cullan, Cullie, Cullin.

Culver (Old English) "dove." Cull, Cully.

Curran (Celtic) "hero." Curry.

Curtis (Old French) "courteous." Curt.

Cutler (Old English) "knifemaker." Cutty.

Cyril (Greek) "lordly." Cy.

Cyrus (Persian) "sun." Russ.

Dale   (Teutonic) "from the valley." Dal.

Dallas   (Celtic) "dweller by the waterfall." Dal.

Dalton   (Old English) "from the farm in the valley." Tony.

Damon   (Greek) "constant; tamer." Damian, Damiano, Damien.

Dana   (Scandinavian) "from Denmark." Dane.

Daniel   (Hebrew) "God is my judge." Dan, Danny.

Darby   (Celtic) "free man." Dar, Derby.

Darcy   (Celtic) "dark." D'Arcy, Dar, Darce.

Darius   (Greek) "wealthy." Derry.

Darnell   (Old English) "from the hidden place." Dar, Darnall.

Darrel   (French) "beloved." Dare, Darrell, Darrill, Darryl.

Darren   (Celtic) "great." Familiar form of Dorian.

David   (Hebrew) "beloved one." Dave, Davey, Davin.

Davis   (Scotch) "son of David."

Dean   (Old English) "from the valley." Deane, Dino.

Delbert   (Teutonic) "bright as day." Del, Bert.

Delmore   (Old French) "from the sea." Del, Delmar, Delmer.

Delwin   (Teutonic) "proud friend." Del, Delwyn.

Dempster   (Old English) "judge."

Denby   (Scandinavian) "from the Danish village." Dennie, Denny.

Denley   (Old English) "from the valley meadow."

Dennis   (Greek) "of Dionysus (god of wine and vegetation)." Dennet, Dennie, Denny, Dion.

Dennison   (Old English) "son of Dennis."

Denton   (Old English) "from the valley farm." Dent.

Derek   (Teutonic) "ruler of the people." Darrick, Derrick, Dirk.

Dermot   (Celtic) "free from envy." Dermott.

Derry   (Celtic) "red-haired."

Desmond   (Celtic) "man from south Munster." Des.

Devin   (Celtic) "poet." Dev.

Devlin   (Celtic) "brave."

Dewey   (Welsh) "prized."

Dewitt   (Old Flemish) "blond." DeWitt, Dwight.

Dexter   (Latin) "dexterous." Dex.

Dillon   (Celtic) "faithful." See also Dylan.

Dinsmore   (Celtic) "from the hill fort." Dinnie, Dinny.

Dominic   (Latin) "belonging to the Lord." Dom, Domingo, Nick, Nicky.

Donahue   (Celtic) "dark warrior." Don, Donohue.

Donald   (Celtic) "dark stranger." Don, Donn, Donny.

Donovan   (Celtic) "dark warrior."

Dorian   (Greek) "from the sea." Darren, Dore, Dorey

Douglas   (Celtic) "from the dark water." Doug, Douglass.

Doyle   (Celtic) "dark stranger."

Drew   (Old French) "sturdy"; (Old Welsh) "wise." Dru.

Duane   (Celtic) "little and dark." Dewain, Dwayne.

Dudley   (Old English) "from the people's meadow."

Duke   (Latin) "leader; duke."

Duncan   (Celtic) "dark-skinned warrior." Dunn.

Dunstan   (Old English) "from the brown stone hill or fortress."

Durant   (Latin) "enduring." Durand.

Durward   (Old English) "gate keeper." Derward, Dur, Ward.

Dustin   (Teutonic) "valiant."

Dylan   (Welsh) "from the sea."

Eligahan

Eamon   Irish form of Edmund.

Earl   (Anglo-Saxon) "nobleman." Earle, Errol, Rollo.

Eaton   (Old English) "from the riverside village."

Ebenezer   (Hebrew) "rock of help." Eb, Eben.

Edna   (Celtic) "fiery."

Edgar   (Anglo-Saxon) "successful spearman." Ed, Eddie, Ned, Ted.

Edmund   (Anglo-Saxon) "prosperous protector." Edmond.

Edsel   (Anglo-Saxon) "from the wealthy man's house."

Edson   (Anglo-Saxon) "son of Edward."

Edward   (Anglo-Saxon) "happy protector." Eduardo.

Edwin   (Anglo-Saxon) "valuable friend." Edlin.

Egan   (Celtic) "ardent." Egon.

Egbert   (Teutonic) "bright as a sword." Bert.

Eldridge   "wise counselor."

Eleazar   (Hebrew) "God has helped." Eli.

Eli   (Hebrew) "the highest."

Elijah   (Hebrew) "Jehovah is God." Eli, Eliot, Elliott. Ellis.

Elisha   (Hebrew) "the Lord is salvation."

Ellery   (Teutonic) "dweller by the older tree." Ellary, Ellerey.

Ellison   "son of Ellis."

Ellsworth   (Teutonic) "nobleman's estate."

Elmer   (Teutonic) "noble; famous."

Elroy   (Latin) "royal."

Elston   (Teutonic) "nobleman's town."

Elton   (Teutonic) "from the old town." Alden, Eldon.

Elwin   (Teutonic) "friend of the elves." Elvis, Elvyn, Elwyn, Win, Winnie.

Elwood   (Teutonic) "from the old wood." Ellwood, Woody.

Emerson   (Teutonic) "son of the industrious ruler."

Emery   (Teutonic) "industrious ruler." Amerigo, Amery, Amory, Emmerich, Emory.

Emil   (Latin) "flattering; winning." Emile, Emlen.

Emmanuel   (Hebrew) "God is with us." Emanuele, Manuel.

Emmett   (Anglo-Saxon) "diligent."

Engelbert   (Teutonic) "bright as an angel." Bert, Ingelbert.

Enoch   (Hebrew) "dedicated."

Enos   (Hebrew) "mortal."

Ephraim   (Hebrew) "doubly fruitful." Efrem, Ephrem.

Erasmus   (Greek) "amiable."

Erastus   (Greek) "beloved."

Erhard (Teutonic) "strong resolution." Erhart.

Eric (Teutonic) "ever-powerful." Erich, Erik, Rick, Ricky.

Ernest (Teutonic) "intent." Ernesto, Ernie, Ernst.

Erskine (Scotch) "from the town of Erskine." Kin, Kinny.

Ethan (Hebrew) "firm."

Etienne French form of Stephen.

Eugene (Greek) "well-born." Gene.

Eustace (Greek) "fruitful." Eustis, Stacy.

Evan (Celtic) "young warrior." Welsh form of John. Ev, Ewen, Owen.

Evelyn (French-Teutonic) From "Avelin," meaning ancestor in German.

Everett (Teutonic) "strong as the wild boar." Eberhard, Everard, Eward, Ewart.

Ezekiel (Hebrew) "strength of God." Zeke.

Ezra (Hebrew) "helper."

Fabian   (Latin) "bean farmer."

Fairfax   (Anglo-Saxon) "fair-haired." Fair, Fax.

Farley   (Old English) "from the bull pasture." Far, Farleigh, Farlie.

Farrell   (Celtic) "man of valor." Farr, Ferrell.

Felix   (Latin) "fortunate." Felice.

Felton   (Old English) "from the farm on the meadow." Felt, Felty.

Fenton   (Old English) "from the marshland farm." Fen, Fenny.

Ferdinand   (Teutonic) "adventurous." Ferd, Fergus, Fernando, Hernando.

Fergus   (Celtic) "strong man."

Ferris   (Celtic) "Peter, the Rock." Irish form of Peter (from Pierce). Farris.

Fidel   (Latin) "faithful."

Fielding   (Old English) "from the field." Field.

Filbert   (Old English) "brilliant." Bert, Phil.

Filmore   (Old English) "famous."

Finlay   (Celtic) "little fair-haired soldier." Findlay, Finn.

Fitzgerald   (Teutonic) "son of the spear-mighty." Fitz, Gerald, Gerry, Jerry.

Fitzhugh   (Teutonic) "son of the intelligent man." Fitz, Hugh.

Fitzpatrick   (Teutonic-Latin) "son of a nobleman." Fitz, Patrick.

Fletcher   (Teutonic) "arrow-featherer; fletcher." Fletch.

Flint   (Teutonic) "stream."

Floyd   (Celtic) "the grey."

Flynn   (Celtic) "son of the red-haired man." Flinn.

Forbes   (Celtic) "prosperous."

Ford   (Old English) "river crossing."

Forrest   (Old French) "forest; woodsman." Forester, Foster.

Francis   (Teutonic) "free." Chico, Fran, Francesco, Franchot, Francisco, Francois, Frank, Frannie, Frans, Franz, Pancho.

Franklin   (Teutonic) "free landowner." See also Francis. Franklyn.

Frazer   (Teutonic) "curly-haired." Fraze, Frazier.

Frederick   (Teutonic) "peaceful ruler." Eric, Erich, Erik, Fred, Frederic, Frederico, Frederik, Fredric, Fredrick, Friedrich, Fritz, Rick, Ricky.

Freeman   (Anglo-Saxon) "free man." Free.

Fremont   (Teutonic) "guardian of freedom." Monty.

Gabriel (Hebrew) "devoted to God." Gabby, Gabe, Gabriele.

Gage (Old French) "pledge."

Gale (Celtic) "stranger"; (Old English) "gay; lively." Gael, Gail, Gayle.

Galen (Celtic) "intelligent." Gaelan.

Galvin (Celtic) "sparrow." Gal, Galvan, Galven.

Gannon (Celtic) "fair-complected."

Gardner (Teutonic) "gardener." Gar, Gard, Gardiner.

Garfield (Teutonic) "battlefield." Gar, Field.

Garland (Teutonic) "wreath." Gar, Garlen.

Garner (Teutonic) "armed sentry." Gar.

Garnett (Teutonic) "armed with a spear"; (Latin) "pomegranate seed; garnet stone." Gar, Garnet.

Garth (Old Norse) "groundskeeper."

Garvey (Celtic) "rough peace." Garv.

Garvin (Teutonic) "comrade in battle." Gar, Garwin, Vin, Vinny, Win, Winny.

Garwood (Teutonic) "from the fir tree forest." Gar, Wood, Woody.

Gary (Teutonic) "spear-carrier." Garry.

Gaston (French) "man from Gascony."

Gavin (Welsh) "white hawk." Gaven, Gawain.

Gaylord   (Old French) "gay lord." Gay, Gaylor.

Gaynor   (Celtic) "son of the fair-complected man." Gainer, Gayner.

Geoffrey   English form of Godfrey; Jeffrey. Geoff, Jeff.

George   (Greek) "farmer." Georg, Giorgio, Jorge.

Gerald   (Teutonic) "mighty with a spear." Gerald, Gary, Gerrie, Gerry, Jerald, Jerrold, Jerry.

Gerard   (Teutonic) "brave with spear." Gerardo, Gerhardt, Gerrie, Gerry.

Gershom   (Hebrew) "exile." Gersham.

Gideon   (Hebrew) "feller of trees; destroyer."

Gifford   (Teutonic) "bold giver."

Gilbert   (Teutonic) "trusted." Bert, Burt, Gib, Gibb, Gil, Wilbert, Wilbur, Wilburt, Will.

Gilchrist   (Celtic) "servant of Christ." Gil, Gill.

Giles   (Greek) "shield-bearer." Gilles.

Gilmore   (Celtic) "servant of the Virgin Mary."

Gilroy   (Celtic) "servant of the red-haired king." Gil, Roy.

Gladwin   (Old English) "cheerful friend." Glad, Win, Winnie.

Glen   (Gaelic) "valley." Glenn, Glyn, Glynn.

Glendon   (Gaelic) "from the dark valley." Glen, Glenn.

Goddard   (Teutonic) "divinely firm." Godard, Godart, Goddart.

Godfrey (Teutonic) "God's peace." Geoffrey, Geoff.

Godwon (Teutonic) "divine friend." Goodwin, Win, Winnie.

Gordon (Old English) "from the triangular hill." Gordie, Gordy.

Grady (Gaelic) "noble; illustrious."

Granger (Old English) "farmer." Grange, Gray.

Grantland (Old English) "from the large meadow." Grant.

Granville (Old French) "from the large town." Gran, Grannie.

Grayson (Old English) "son of a bailiff." Gray, Son, Sonny.

Gregory (Greek) "watchman." Greg, Gregg, Gregor, Gregorio.

Griffin (Latin) "griffin (a mythical beast)." Griff.

Griffith (Old Welsh) "fierce chief."

Griswold (Teutonic) "from the gray forest."

Grover (Old English) "from the grove."

Gunther (Old Norse) "warrior." Gun, Gunnar, Gunner, Gunter.

Gustave (Swedish) "staff of the Goths." Gus, Gustaf, Gustav.

Guthrie (Celtic) "war serpent."

Guy (French) "guide"; (Teutonic) "warrior"; (Celtic) "sensible."

Hadley   (Old English) "from the heath." Had, Lee, Leigh.

Haldan   (Teutonic) "half-Danish." Dan, Danny, Don, Donny, Hal.

Hale   (Teutonic) "robust." Hal.

Haley   (Gaelic) "ingenious." Hal, Hale, Lee, Leigh.

Hall   (Old English) "from the hall."

Halsey   (Old English) "from Hal's island." Hal.

Halstead   (Old English) "from the manor." Hal, Halsted.

Hamilton   (Norman) "from the beautiful mountain." Ham, Hamil, Tony.

Hamlin   (Teutonic) "ruler of the home." Ham, Lin, Lynn.

Harcourt   (Old French) "fortified dwelling." Harry, Court.

Hardy   (Teutonic) "bold and daring."

Harlan   (Teutonic) "from the land of warriors." Harland, Harlin.

Harley   (Old English) "from the meadow." Arley.

Harlow   (Old English) "from the rough hill." Arlo.

Harmon   English form of Herman.

Harold   (Teutonic) "army-ruler." Hal, Harry.

Harper   (Old English) "harp player." Harp.

Harrison   (Old English) "son of Harry." Harris.

Hartley   (Old English) "from the deer meadow." Hart.

Harvey (Teutonic) "warrior." Harv, Herve, Hervey.

Haslett (Teutonic) "from the hazel tree land." Haze, Hazlett.

Hastings (Teutonic) "son of stern man." Hastie, Hasty.

Hayden (Old English) "from the hedged hill." Haydon.

Hayes (Old English) "from the hedged place."

Haywood (Old English) "from the hedged forest." Heywood, Woodie, Woody.

Heath (Middle English) "from the heath."

Hector (Greek) "steadfast."

Henry (Teutonic) "ruler of an estate." Enrico, Hal, Hank, Harry, Heinrich, Hendrik, Henri.

Herbert (Teutonic) "bright soldier." Bert, Bertie, Harbert, Hebert, Herb, Herbie.

Herman (Teutonic) "warrior." Armand, Armin, Harmon, Hermann.

Hernando Spanish form of Ferdinand.

Hershel (Hebrew) "deer." Herschel, Hersh, Hirsch.

Hewett (Teutonic) "little and intelligent." Hewitt.

Hilary (Latin) "cheerful." Hi, Hilaire, Hill, Hillary, Hillie, Hilly.

Hillard (Teutonic) "brave warrior." Hill, Hillyer.

Hiram (Hebrew) "exalted." Hy.

Hobart (Teutonic) "bright-minded." Hobard.

Holbrook   (Old English) "from the brook in the hollow." Brook, Holbrooke.

Holde.·   (Teutonic) "gracious."

Hollis   (Old English) "from the grove of holly trees."

Holmes   (Teutonic) "from the river islands."

Holt   (Old English) "from the forest."

Homer   (Greek) "promise."

Horace   (Latin) "keeper of the hours." Horatio.

Hosea   (Hebrew) "salvation."

Howard   (Teutonic) "watchman." Howie, Ward.

Howland   (Old English) "from the hills."

Hubert   (Teutonic) "bright-minded." Bert, Hobart, Huberto, Hubie, Hugh, Hugo.

Hugh   (Teutonic) "intelligence." Huey, Hughie, Hugo.

Humbert   (Teutonic) "brilliant Hun." Hum.

Humphrey   (Teutonic) "peaceful Hun." Hum, Humfrey, Onofredo.

Hunter   (Old English) "hunter." Hunt.

Huntington   (Old English) "hunting estate." Hunt, Huntingdon.

Huntley   (Old English) "hunter's meadow." Hunt, Lee, Leigh.

Hurley   (Celtic) "sea-tide."

Huxley   (Old English) "from Hugh's meadow." Hux, Lee, Leigh.

Hyatt   (Old English) "from the high gate."

Hyman   English form of Chaim. Hy, Manny.

Ian   Scotch form of John.

Ignatius   (Latin) "fiery; ardent." Iggy, Ignance, Ignacio.

Ingemar   (Old Norse) "famous son." Ingamar, Ingmar.

Inger   (Old Norse) "son's army." Igor, Ingar.

Innis   (Celtic) "from the island." Inness.

Ira   (Hebrew) "descendant."

Irving   (Celtic) "beautiful"; (Old English) "sea friend." Erv, Ervin, Erwin, Irv, Irwin.

Isaac   (Hebrew) "he who laughs." Ike, Isaak.

Isadore   (Greek) "gift of Isis." Dore, Dory.

Isaiah   (Hebrew) "salvation of God." Isa.

Israel   (Hebrew) "soldier for the Lord."

Ivan   Russian form of John.

Ivar   (Scandinavian) "archer." Iver, Ivor.

Jackson   (Old English) "son of Jack." Jack.

Jacob   (Hebrew) "supplanter." Cobb, Jack, Jacques, Jaime, Jake, Jamie, Jay, Jayme, Jim, Jimmie, Jimmy, Seamus, Shamus.

Jacques   French form of Jacob; James.

Jaime   Spanish form of James. Jayme.

James   English form of Jacob (from Jaime). Jacques, Jaime, Jamie, Jay, Jayme, Jim, Jimmy, Seamus, Shamus.

Jan   Dutch and Slavic form of John. Janos.

Jared   Hebrew form of Jordan. Jerad.

Jarvis   (Teutonic) "keen as a spear." Jervis.

Jason   (Greek) "healer." Jay.

Jasper   English form of Casper (from Gaspar).

Jean   French form of John.

Jed   (Hebrew) "beloved of the Lord." A short form of Jedidiah. Jedd.

Jefferson   (Old English) "son of Jeffrey." Jeff, Jeffie.

Jeffrey   (Old French) "heavenly peace." Geoff, Geoffrey, Godfrey, Gottfried, Jeff, Jefferey.

Jeremiah   (Hebrew) "appointed by Jehovah." Jere, Jereme, Jeremy, Jerry.

Jerome   (Latin) "holy name." Gerrie, Gerry, Jere, Jereme, Jerry.

Jesse   (Hebrew) "gift of God." Jess, Jessie.

Jethro   (Hebrew) "preeminence." Jeth.

Joachim (Hebrew) "the Lord will judge." Joaquin.

Joel (Hebrew) "Jehovah is God."

John (Hebrew) "God's precious gift." Evan, Ewen, Hans, Ian, Jack, Jackie, Jan, Janos, Jean, Jens, Jock, Jocko, Johann, Johannes, Johnnie, Johnny, Jon, Juan, Owen, Sean, Shaun, Shawn, Zane.

Jonah (Hebrew) "dove." Jonas.

Jonathan (Hebrew) "Jehovah gave." Jon, Jonathon.

Jordan (Hebrew) "descender." Jared, Jerad, Jourdain.

Joseph (Hebrew) "he shall add." Che, Giuseppe, Jo, Joe, Joey, Jose.

Joshua (Hebrew) "Jehovah saves." Josh.

Josiah (Hebrew) "Jehovah supports."

Joyce (Teutonic) "of the Goths." Jocelyn.

Judah (Hebrew) "praised." Jud, Judd, Jude.

Jules French form of Julius. Jule.

Julian (Latin) "belonging or related to Julius."

Julius (Greek) "youthful and downy-bearded." Jule, Jules, Julie.

Justin (Latin) "upright." Justinian, Justis, Justus.

Kane (Celtic) "fair; bright." Kain, Kaine, Kayne.

Karl German form of Charles.

Keane (Old English) "sharp; keen." See also Keenan. Kean, Keene.

Kearney Form of Carney.

Keefe (Celtic) "cherished; handsome."

Keegan (Celtic) "fiery."

Keenan (Celtic) "little and ancient." Keen, Kienan.

Kein (Celtic) "dark-skinned."

Keith (Welsh) "wood-dweller."

Kelly (Celtic) "warrior." Kelley.

Kelsey (Teutonic) "dweller by the water."

Kendall (Celtic) "from the bright valley." Ken, Kendal, Kendell, Kenny.

Kendrick (Anglo-Saxon) "son of Henry"; (Old English) "royal ruler." Ken, Rick.

Kennedy (Celtic) "helmeted chief."

Kenneth (Celtic) "handsome"; (Old English) "royal oath." Ken, Kenny.

Kent (Welsh) "white, bright." Short form of Kenton.

Kenton (Old English) "from the farm in Kent." Ken, Kenn, Kent.

Kenyon (Gaelic) "white-haired; blond."

Kermit (Celtic) "free man." Ker, Kerr.

Kerry (Celtic) "dark."

Kevin (Celtic) "gentle; kind."

Killian (Celtic) "little and warlike." Killian, Killy.

Kim (Welsh) "chief."

Kimball (Anglo-Saxon) "warrior chief; royal and bold."

Kingsley (Old English) "from the king's meadow." King, Kinsely.

Kingston (Old English) "from the king's manor."

Kipp (Old English) "from the pointed hill."

Kirby (Teutonic) "from the church village."

Kirk (Teutonic) "from the church."

Kit Familiar form of Christopher.

Knute Danish form of Canute.

Kurt German form of Conrad.

Kyle (Celtic) "handsome; from the strait." Ky.

Ladd   (Middle English) "attendant." Lad, Laddie.

Laird   (Scotch) "landed proprietor; laird."

Lamar   (Teutonic) "famous throughout the land."

Lambert   (Teutonic) "bright as the land." Bert, Lamberto.

Lamont   (Scandinavian) "lawyer." Lammond, Monty.

Lance   (Teutonic) "land." Lancelot.

Lane   (Old English) "from the narrow road." Lanie.

Langdon   (Old English) "from the long hill." Landon, Langston.

Latham   (Teutonic) "dweller and the barn."

Lathrop   (Old English) "from the village of barns."

Latimer   (Anglo-French) "interpreter." Lat, Latty.

Lawford   (Old English) "from the ford on the hill." Law, Ford.

Lawrence   (Latin) "laurel-crowned." Larry, Lars, Lauren, Laurence, Laurens, Laurent, Laurie, Lon, Lonny, Loren, Lorenzo, Lorin, Lorrie, Lorry, Rance.

Lawton   (Old English) "from the estate on the hill."

Lazarus   (Hebrew) "God will help." Lazar.

Leander   (Greek) "lionlike." Ander, Lee, Leigh, Leo.

Leif   (Old Norse) "beloved." Lief.

Leighton   (Old English) "from the meadow farm."

Leland   (Old English) "from the meadow land." Lee, Leigh.

Lemuel   (Hebrew) "dedicated to the Lord." Lem.

Leo   (Latin) "lion." Short form of Leander; Leonard; Leopold. Lee, Leon, Lev.

Leon   (French) "lion; lionlike." French form of Leo. Short form of Leonard; Napoleon. Léon.

Leonard   (Teutonic) "bold lion." See also Leander. Lee, Len, Lenny, Leo, Leon, Lonny.

Leopold   (Teutonic) "patriotic."

Leroy   (French-Latin) "royal." Elroy, Lee, Leigh, Roy.

Leslie   (Celtic) "from the gray fort." Lee, Leigh, Les.

Lester   (Latin) "from the camp of the legion"; (Old English) "from Leicester."

Levi   (Hebrew) "united."

Lewis   Short form of Llewellyn. Form of Louis. Lew.

Lincoln   (Celtic-Latin) "from the settlement by the pool." Linc, Link.

Lindsay   (Old English) "from the island of serpents." Lind, Lindsey.

Linus   (Greek) "flaxen-haired."

Lionel   (Latin) "lionlike."

Llewellyn   (Celtic) "lionlike; ruler." Lew, Lewis.

Lloyd   (Celtic) "gray." Floyd, Loy.

Locke   (Old English) "from the forest." Lock.

Logan   (Celtic) "from the hollow."

Lombard   (Teutonic) "long-bearded." Bard, Barr.

Lorimer   (Latin) "harness-maker." Lorrie, Lorrimer, Lorry.

Loring   (Old High German) "son of the famous warrior." Lorrie, Lorry.

Louis   (Teutonic) "renowned warrior." Aloysius, Lew, Lewis, Lou, Louie, Ludwig, Luigi, Luis.

Lowell   (Old English) "beloved." Lovell, Lowe.

Lucius   (Latin) "bringer of light." Lucas, Lucias, Lucian, Lukas, Luke.

Luther   (Teutonic) "famous warrior."

Lyle   (French-Latin) "from the island." Lisle.

Lyman   (Old English) "a man from the valley."

Lyndon   (Teutonic) "from the linden tree hill." Lin, Lindon, Lindy, Lyn, Lynn.

Lynn   (Old English) "dweller by the waterfall." Lin, Linn, Lyn.

Mac (Celtic) "son of." Short form of names beginning with "mac"; "max"; "mc." Mack.

Mackenzie (Celtic) "son of the wise leader." Mac, Mack.

Macklin (Celtic) "son of Flann, the red-haired."

Macnair (Celtic) "son of the heir."

Maddox (Celtic) "beneficent."

Madison (Teutonic) "son of the mighty soldier." Maddie, Sonny.

Magnus (Latin) "great." Manus.

Major (Latin) "greater." Mayer, Mayor.

Malachi (Hebrew) "angel." Mal, Malachy.

Malcolm (Celtic) "follower of St. Columba (an early Scottish saint)." Mal.

Mallory (Teutonic) "army counselor." Mal.

Manfred (Teutonic) "man of peace." Fred, Freddie, Mannie, Manny.

Marcel (Latin) "little and warlike." Marcellus.

Mark (Latin) "hammer." Marc, Marcos, Marcus, Mario, Marius.

Marlow (Old English) "from the hill by the lake." Marlowe.

Marshall (Old French) "steward; horse-keeper." Marsh, Marshal.

Martin (Latin) "warlike." Martie, Martino, Marty.

Marvin (Teutonic) "lover of the sea." Marve, Marwin, Mervin, Merwin, Merwyn.

Mason   (French-Teutonic) "stone-worker." Mace, Sonny.

Matthew   (Hebrew) "gift of God." Mathias, Matt, Matthias, Mattie, Matty.

Maurice   (Latin) "dark-skinned." Maurie, Maury, Morey, Morris.

Max   Short form of Maximilian.

Maximilian   (Latin) "the greatest." Mac, Mack, Max, Maxie.

Maxwell   (Anglo-Saxon) "from the rich man's well."

Maynard   (Teutonic) "powerful; brave." May, Mayne, Menard.

Mead   (Old English) "from the meadow." Meade.

Melbourne   (Old English) "from the mill stream." Mel, Melburn.

Melville   (Old English-French) "from the estate of the hard worker." Mel.

Melvin   (Celtic) "chief." Mel, Melvyn, Vinnie.

Mendel   (Greek) "knowledge; wisdom." Mendy.

Meredith   (Old Welsh) "protection from the sea." Merideth, Merry.

Merlin   (French-Latin) "falcon." Marlin, Marlon, Merle.

Merrill   (Teutonic) "famous." Merill, Meryl.

Meyer   (Teutonic) "farmer." Meier, Meir, Myer.

Michael   (Hebrew) "like unto the Lord." Micah, Michal, Michail, Michele, Mickey, Miguel, Mike, Mischa, Mitch, Mitchel, Mitchell.

Miles   (Latin) "soldier." Milo, Myles.

Millard   (Latin) "keeper of the mill."

Milton   (Old English) "from the mill town." Milt.

Monroe   (Celtic) "from the mouth of the Roe River." Munroe.

Montague   (French) "from the pointed mountain." Monte, Monty.

Montgomery   (Old English) "from the rich man's mountain." Monte, Monty.

Mordecai   (Hebrew) "belonging to Marduk." Mord, Mordy, Mort, Mortie.

Morris   (Latin) "dark-skinned."

Mortimer   (French-Latin) "dweller by the still water." Mort.

Moses   (Hebrew) "saved from the water." Moise, Mose, Moshe, Moss.

Muhammad   (Arabic) "praised." A Muslim saying: "If you have a hundred sons, name them all Muhammad." There are more than 500 variations of this name; it is the most common boy's name in the world.

Murdock   (Celtic) "wealthy seaman."

Murray   (Celtic) "sailor."

Myron   (Greek) "fragrant ointment." Ron, Ronnie.

Napoleon (Italian) "from Naples." Leon, Nap, Napoleon, Nappie, Nappy.

Nathaniel (Hebrew) "gift of God." Nat, Nate, Nathan, Nathanael.

Nehemiah (Hebrew) "comforted by the Lord."

Neil (Celtic) "champion." Neal, Neale, Neill, Neils, Nels, Niel, Niels, Niles, Nils.

Nelson (English) "son of Neil." Nealson, Neils, Nels, Niles, Nils, Nilson.

Nestor (Greek) "wisdom."

Neville (Latin) "from the new town." Nev, Nevil.

Nevin (Celtic) "worshipper of the saint"; (Teutonic) "nephew." Nevins, Niven.

Newlin (Celtic) "from the new spring."

Newton (Anglo-Saxon) "from the new farmstead."

Nicholas (Greek) "the people's victory." Claus, Cole, Colin, Niccolo, Nick, Nicky, Nicol, Nicolai, Nicolas, Nikita, Nikki.

Nigel (Latin) "dark."

Noah (Hebrew) "rest."

Noel (French-Latin) "born at Christmas."

Nolan (Celtic) "famous; noble." Noland.

Norbert (Teutonic) "brilliant hero." Bert, Bertie, Norb.

Norman (Teutonic) "man from the north." Norm.

Norris (French-Latin) "caretaker."

Northrop   (Anglo-Saxon) "from the north farm."

Norton   (Anglo-Saxon) "from the northern village."

Norwood   (Teutonic) "guardian of the north gate."

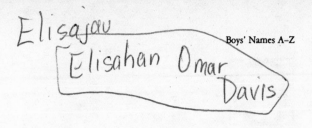

Oakes   (Old English) "from the oak trees." Oak, Oakley.

Obadiah   (Hebrew) "servant of God." Obie.

Odell   (Norse) "man of property." Dell, Ody.

Ogden   (Old English) "from the oak tree valley."

Olaf   (Old Norse) "ancestral talisman relic." Olav, Ole, Olen, Olin.

Oliver   (Latin) "olive tree symbolizing peace." Noll, Olivero, Olivier, Ollie.

Omar   (Arabic) "first son; follower of the Prophet."

Ordway   (Anglo-Saxon) "warrior with spear."

Oren   (Celtic) "pale." Oran, Orin, Orren, Orrin.

Orestes   (Greek) "mountain man."

Orion   (Celtic) "son of fire."

Orland   (Teutonic) "from the famed land." Land, Lanny, Orlan, Orlando.

Ormond   (Teutonic) "mariner."

Orson   (Latin) "bearlike; strong." Sonny.

Orton   (Teutonic) "wealthy."

Orville   (Old French) "from the golden estate." Ory.

Osborn   (Teutonic) "divine bear." Osbourne, Ozzie.

Oscar   (Celtic) "leaping spearman." Askar, Ozzie.

Osgood   (Teutonic) "divine creator."

Osmond   (Teutonic) "divine protector." Osmund.

Oswald   (Teutonic) "having power from God." Oswell, Ozzie, Waldo.

Otis   (Greek) "keen of hearing." Oates.

Otto   (Teutonic) "prosperous." Othello.

Owen   (Celtic) "young warrior."

Oxford   (Old English) "from the river crossing of the oxen." Ford.

Page   (French) "youthful attendant." Padgett, Paige.

Palmer   (Old English) "palm-bearing pilgrim."

Parker   (Middle English) "guardian of the park." Park, Parke.

Parnell   (French) "little Peter." Nell.

Parrish   (Middle English) "from the churchyard." Parry.

Pascal   (Italian) "born at Easter or Passover." Pascale, Pasquale.

Patrick   (Latin) "nobleman." Paddy, Padriac, Pat, Paton, Patrice, Patsy, Patty.

Patton   (Old English) "from the warrior's estate." Pat, Patin, Paton, Patten, Pattin, Patty.

Paul   (Latin) "small." Pablo, Paulie.

Pembroke   (Welsh) "from the headland."

Penn   (Teutonic) "commander." Short form of Penrod. Pennie, Penny.

Penrod   (Teutonic) "famous commander." Pen, Penn, Rod, Roddy.

Percival   (Old French) "pierce-the-valley"; (Greek) "destroyer." Percy.

Perry   (Old English) "pear tree"; (Old French) "little Peter."

Peter   (Greek) "rock." Farris, Ferris, Parry, Pedro, Peirce, Perkin, Perry, Pete, Pierce, Pierre, Pietro.

Peyton   (Old English) "from the warrior's estate." Payton.

Phelps   (Old English) "son of Philip."

Philip   (Greek) "lover of horses." Felipe, Phil, Phillip, Phillipe.

Phinens (Hebrew) "oracle."

Pierrepont (French-Latin) "dweller by the stone bridge."

Plato (Greek) "broad-shouldered."

Pomeroy (Old French) "from the apple orchard." Pom, Roy.

Porter (Latin) "keeper of the gate."

Prentice (Latin) "apprentice; learner." Pren.

Prescott (Old English) "from the priest's cottage." Scott, Scotty.

Preston (Old English) "from the priest's estate."

Price (Welsh) "son of the ardent one." Brice, Bryce.

Primo (Italian) "firstborn."

Pryor (Latin) "head of a monastery; prior." Pry.

Quentin   (Latin) "fifth child." Quent, Quinn, Quint.

Quillan   (Celtic) "cub." Quill.

Quinby   (Scandinavian) "from the woman's estate."

Quincy   (Old French) "from the fifth son's estate."

Quinlan   (Celtic) "physically strong."

Radburn　(Old English) "from the red stream." Rad, Radborne, Radbourne.

Radcliffe　(Old English) "from the red cliff." Rad, Cliff.

Rafael　Spanish form of Raphael. Rafe.

Rafferty　(Celtic) "prosperous." Rafe.

Raleigh　(Old English) "from the deer meadow." Lee, Leigh, Rawley.

Ralph　(Old English) "protector." Rolph.

Ramòn　Spanish form of Raymond.

Ramsay　(Teutonic) "from the ram's island; from the raven's island." Ram, Ramsey.

Randall　Modern form of Randolph. Rand, Randell, Randy.

Randolph　(Teutonic) "shield-wolf." Rand, Randall, Randell, Randolf, Randy.

Ransom　(Old English) "son of the shield."

Raphael　(Hebrew) "divine healer." Rafael, Rafe, Ray.

Rayburn　(Old English) "from the deer brook." Burn, Burny, Ray.

Raymond　(Teutonic) "mighty or wise protector." Raimundo, Ramòn, Ray, Raymund.

Redford　(Old English) "from the red river crossing." Ford, Red.

Reece　(Welsh) "enthusiastic." Rhys, Rice, Rhett.

Reed　(Old English) "red-haired." Reade, Reid.

Reeve　(Middle English) "steward."

Regan (Celtic) "kingly." Reagan, Reagen.

Reginald (Teutonic) "powerful and mighty." Reg, Reggie, Reinald, Reinhold, Renault, René, Reynolds, Rinaldo.

Remington (Teutonic) "from the raven estate." Tony.

René (French) "reborn." French short form of Reginald.

Renfred (Teutonic) "peacemaker."

Reuben (Greek) "behold, a son." Rube, Ruben, Rubin.

Rex (Latin) "king."

Reynard (Old French) "fox." Ray, Raynard, Reinhard, Renard, Renaud, Rey.

Richard (Teutonic) "powerful ruler." Dick, Ric, Ricardo, Rich, Richie, Rick, Ricki, Ricky, Rico, Riki.

Richmond (Teutonic) "mighty protector."

Ridley (Old English) "from the red meadow."

Riley (Celtic) "valiant." Reilly.

Riordan (Celtic) "royal poet." Dan, Danny.

Ripley (Anglo-Saxon) "from the shouter's meadow." Lee, Leigh, Rip.

Roarke (Celtic) "famous ruler."

Robert (Teutonic) "bright fame." Bob, Bobby, Rab, Rip, Rob, Robb, Robbie, Robby, Roberto, Robin, Rupert.

Robinson (English) "son of Robert." Robin.

Rochester (Teutonic) "from the stone camp." Chester, Chet, Rocky.

Rockwell (Old English) "from the rocky spring."

Roderick (Teutonic) "famous ruler." Rod, Roddy, Roderic, Rodrigo, Rodrique, Rory.

Rodman (Old English) "dweller by the cross." Rod, Roddy.

Rodney (Teutonic) "famous."

Roger (Teutonic) "famous spearman." Rodge, Rodger, Rog, Rogers, Rutger.

Roland (Teutonic) "from the famous land." Lanny, Rollie, Rollins, Rollo, Rowland.

Roman (Latin) "from Rome." Romain.

Romeo (Italian) "pilgrim to Rome."

Rooney (Celtic) "red-haired." Rowan, Rowen.

Rory (Celtic) "red king."

Roscoe (Teutonic) "from the deer forest." Ross, Coe.

Ross (Old French) "red"; (Scotch Gaelic) "headland."

Roy (Old French) "king."

Royal (Old French) "kingly."

Royce (Old English) "son of the king."

Rudolph (Teutonic) "famous wolf." Raoul, Rolf, Rolfe, Rollo, Rudie, Rudolf, Rudy.

Rudyard (Old English) "from the red enclosure." Rudd, Rudy.

Rufus (Latin) "red-haired." Rufe.

Russell   (Latin) "red-haired; fox-colored."

Rutherford   (Old English) "from the cattle ford." Ford.

Rutledge   (Old English) "from the red pool."

Ryan   (Irish Gaelic) "little king."

Salvatore (Italian) "savior." Sal.

Samson (Hebrew) "resplendent." Sam, Sammy, Sansome.

Samuel (Hebrew) "asked of God." Sam, Samuele, Shem.

Sanborn (Old English) "from the sandy brook." Sandy.

Sancho (Latin) "sanctified."

Sanders (Greek) "son of Alexander." Sandor, Saunders.

Sanford (Old English) "from the sandy cord." Sandy.

Sargent (Old French-Latin) "army officer." Sarge, Sergeant, Sergent.

Saul (Hebrew) "longed for." Sol, Solly, Zolly.

Sawyer (Celtic) "sawer of wood."

Saxon (Old English) "swordsman." Sax.

Schuyler (Dutch) "scholar." Sky.

Scott (Old English) "Scotsman." Scot, Scottie.

Seamus Irish form of James. Shamus.

Sean Irish form of John. Shane, Shaun, Shawn.

Searle (Teutonic) "wearing armor."

Sebastian (Greek) "revered." Bastien, Sebastien.

Selby (Teutonic) "from the manor farm."

Seldon (Teutonic) "from the valley." Don, Donny.

Selwyn (Anglo-Saxon) "friend from the palace." Selwin, Winnie, Wynn.

Serge (Latin) "attendant." Sergio.

Seth (Hebrew) "the appointed."

Seward (Anglo-Saxon) "guardian of the seacoast."

Seymour (Old French) "from St. Maur." Morey, Morrie.

Shannon (Celtic) "small and wise."

Shaw (Old English) "from the shady grove."

Sheehan (Celtic) "little and peaceful."

Sheffield (Old English) "from the crooked field." Field, Sheff.

Shelby (Anglo-Saxon) "from the ledge farm." Shell, Shelly.

Sheldon (Old English) "from the farm on the ledge." Shell, Shelley, Shelton.

Sheridan (Celtic) "wild man."

Sherlock (Old English) "fair-haired."

Sherman (Old English) "shearer." Manny, Sherm.

Sherwin (Old English) "swift runner." Win, Winnie.

Sherwood (Old English) "from the bright forest." Wood, Woody.

Sidney (Old French) "from St. Denys." Sid.

Siegfried (Teutonic) "victorious peace." Sig, Sigfrid.

Sigmund (Teutonic) "victorious protector." Sig.

Silas (Latin) "man of the forest." Silvain, Sylvan.

Simon (Hebrew) "he who hears." Si, Simeon, Simone.

Sinclair (Old French) "from St. Clair." Clair, Clare.

Sloan (Celtic) "warrior." Sloane.

Solomon (Hebrew) "peaceful." Sol, Solly.

Spencer (Old English-Latin) "dispenser of provisions." Spence.

Sprague (Teutonic) "lively."

Stacy (Latin) "stable; dependable."

Stanfield (Old English) "from the stony field."

Stanford (Old English) "from the landing ford." Stan, Ford.

Stanislaus (Slavonic) "glory of the camp." Stan, Stanislaw.

Stanley (Old English) "dweller at stony meadow." Stan.

Stanton (Old English) "from the stone dwelling."

Stephen (Greek) "crown." Etienne, Esteban, Stefan, Stefano, Stephan, Steve, Steven.

Sterling (Old English) "of honest value."

Stillman (Anglo-Saxon) "quiet man."

Stuart (Old English) "caretaker; steward." Steward, Stewart, Stu.

Sullivan (Celtic) "black-eyed."

Sumner (French-Latin) "church officer; summoner."

Sutton   (Old English) "from the south village."

Sven   (Old Norse) "youth." Swen.

Sylvester   (Latin) "from the woods."

Tab (Spanish-Arabic) "drummer." Tabb, Tabby.

Talbot (Old French) "valley-bright."

Tanner (Old English) "leather worker; tanner." Tann, Tanny.

Tate (Middle English) "cheerful."

Tavish (Celtic) "twin." Tavis, Tevis.

Taylor (French-Latin) "tailor."

Teague (Celtic) "bard."

Templeton (Old English) "from the town of the temple." Temp, Temple.

Terence (Latin) "tender"; (Celtic) "like a tall tower." Terrence, Terry.

Thaddeus (Greek) "courageous"; (Hebrew) "the praised." Tad, Tadd, Thad.

Thatcher (Old English) "roofer; thatcher." Thaxter.

Thayer (Teutonic) "from the nation's army."

Theobald (Teutonic) "patriotic." Ted, Tedd, Teddy, Thébault, Theo.

Theodore (Greek) "divine gift." Ted, Tedd, Teddy.

Theodoric (Teutonic) "ruler of the people." Derek, Dirk, Dieter, Dietrich.

Thomas (Hebrew) "twin." Tam, Tammy, Thoma, Tom, Tomaso, Tomkin, Tomlin, Tommie, Tommy.

Thorndike (Old English) "from the thorny embankment." Thorn.

Thornton (Old English) "from the thorn tree farm." Thorn.

Thorpe (Teutonic) "from the hamlet."

Thurston   (Scandinavian) "Thor's stone or jewel."

Timothy   (Greek) "honoring God." Tim, Timmie, Timmy.

Titus   (Greek) "giant"; (Latin) "safe." Tito.

Tobias   (Hebrew) "goodness of the Lord." Tobe, Tobie, Tobin, Toby.

Todd   (Middle English) "fox."

Torrance   (Celtic) "from the tower." Torey, Torr, Torrence, Torry.

Townsend   (Old English) "from the town's end." Town, Townie.

Tracy   (Celtic) "battler"; (Latin) "courageous." Tracey.

Trahern   (Celtic) "strong as iron." Tray.

Travis   (French-Latin) "from the crossroads." Traver, Travers.

Trent   (Latin) "dweller by the river front."

Trevor   (Celtic) "prudent." Trev.

Tristan   (Latin) "sorrowful." Tris, Tristram.

Troy   (Celtic) "foot soldier."

Truman   (Old English) "faithful man."

Tucker   (Old English) "tucker of cloth." Tuck.

Tyler   (Old English) "maker of tiles."

Tynan   (Celtic) "dark." Ty.

Tyrone   (Greek) "sovereign"; (Celtic) "land of Owen." Ty.

Tyrus English form of Thor. Ty.

Tyson (Teutonic) "son of the Teuton."

Udell   (Old English) "from the yew tree valley." Del, Dell.

Uland   (Teutonic) "from the noble land."

Ulric   (Teutonic) "wolf-ruler." Ric, Rick, Ricky, Ulrick.

Ulysses   (Greek) "wrathful." Ulick, Ulises.

Upton   (Anglo-Saxon) "from the upper town."

Urban   (Latin) "from the city; courteous."

Uriah   (Hebrew) "Jehovah is my light."

Vail   (French-Latin) "from the valley."

Valentine   (Latin) "strong; healthy." Val.

Van   (Dutch) "from." Short form of many Dutch surnames.

Vance   (Middle English) "thresher."

Vaughn   (Celtic) "small." Vaughan.

Vernon   (Latin) "flourishing." Lavern, Vern, Verne.

Victor   (Latin) "conqueror." Vic, Vick.

Vincent   (Latin) "conquering." Vin, Vince, Vincenz, Vinnie, Vinny.

Virgil   (Latin) "blooming."

Vito   (Latin) "alive."

Vladimir   (Slavonic) "world ruler."

Volney   (Teutonic) "of the people."

Wade   (Anglo-Saxon) "wanderer."

Wainwright   (Old English) "wagonmaker." Wayne, Wright.

Waite   (Old English) "guard."

Wakefield   (Old English) "from the wet field." Field, Wake.

Waldemar   (Teutonic) "powerful and famous." Waldo, Wally.

Waldo   (Teutonic) "ruler." Familar form of Oswald; Waldemar.

Walker   (Old English) "thickener of cloth."

Wallace   (Teutonic) "Welshman." Wallis, Wally, Walsh, Welch, Welsh.

Walter   (Teutonic) "mighty warrior." Gauthier, Walt, Walther.

Walton   (Old English) "from the walled town." Wally, Walt.

Ward   (Teutonic) "guardian." Warden, Worden.

Warner   (Teutonic) "guarding warrior." Werner.

Warren   (Teutonic) "game warden." Waring.

Washburn   (Old English) "from near the overflowing brook." Burn, Burnie.

Washington   (Old English) "from the town of one known for astuteness."

Watson   (Teutonic) "son of Walter."

Wayland   (Old English) "from the land by the highway." Land, Way, Waylen.

Wayne   (Old English) "wagoner." Short form of Wainwright.

Webster   (Old English) "weaver." Webb.

Wells (Old English) "dweller by the springs."

Wendell (Teutonic) "wanderer." Wendel.

Wesley (Old English) "from the western meadow." Lee, Leigh, Wes.

Westbrook (Old English) "from the western brook." Wes, West, Brook, Brooke.

Weston (Old English) "from the western farmstead." Wes, West.

Wheeler (Old English) "wheelmaker."

Whitman (Old English) "white-haired man." Whit.

Whitney (Old English) "from the white island." Whit.

Whittaker (Old English) "from the white field." Whit.

Wilbur (Anglo-Saxon) "beloved stronghold." Wilbert, Wilburt.

Wiley (Old English) "from the water meadow." Wylie.

Wilfred (Teutonic) "resolute and peaceful." Wilfrid, Will, Willie, Willy.

Willard (Teutonic) "resolutely brave." Will, Willie, Willy.

William (Teutonic) "determined guardian." Bill, Billy, Wilhelm, Will, Willi, Willie, Willis, Wilmer.

Wilmot (Teutonic) "beloved heart."

Wilton (Old English) "from the farm by the spring." Will, Willie, Wilt.

Winfield (Old English) "from the friendly field." Field, Win, Winnie, Winny.

Winfred (Teutonic) "friend of peace."

Winslow   (Old English) "from the friend's hill." Win, Winnie, Winny.

Winston   (Old English) "from the friendly town." Win, Winnie, Winny.

Winthrop   (Old English) "from the friendly village." Win, Winnie, Winny.

Wolfgang   (Teutonic) "advancing wolf." Wolf.

Woodrow   (Old English) "from the hedgerow in the forest." Wood, Woody.

Worth   (Old English) "from the farmstead."

Wright   (Anglo-Saxon) "carpenter."

Wyatt   (Old French) "guide."

Wylie   (Old English) "charming." Lee, Leigh, Wiley.

Wynn   (Old Welsh) "fair." Winnie.

Xanthus   (Latin) "golden-haired."

Xavier   (Arabic) "bright." Javier.

Xenophon   (Greek) "strange voice." Zennie.

Xenos   (Greek) "stranger."

Xerxes   (Persian) "ruler." Zerk.

Xylon   (Greek) "from the forest."

Yale   (Old English) "from the corner of the land."

Yancy   (American Indian) "Englishman." Yance, Yank, Yankee.

Yardley   (Old English) "from the enclosed meadow." Lee, Leigh, Yard.

Yehudi   (Hebrew) "praise of the Lord."

York   (Old English) "estate of the boar."

Yule   (Old English) "born at Yuletide." Yul.

Yves   French form of Ivar. Ives.

Zachary   (Hebrew) "remembered by the Lord." Zach, Zachariah, Zacharias, Zacharie, Zak, Zeke.

Zebulon   (Hebrew) "dwelling place." Zeb.

Zedekiah   (Hebrew) "God is mighty and just." Zed.

Chapter 9

What Was Your Name, Again: Pseudonyms And Nicknames

In the next few pages we'll take a look at a broad cross section of luminaries who have, for one reason or another, changed their names—acquiring a pseudonym—or been graced with a nickname by family or associates. (That's the distinction between the two: one chooses a pseudonym; one is given a nickname by others.)

People with pseudonyms listed include the famous and infamous, the admired and the despised. Most are actors and writers who selected more pleasing or appropriate titles than those their parents bequeathed them. But they all share a common characteristic: the "new" names they adopted became well-known in most American households during their lifetimes.

The nicknames we cite are also those of famous persons. Yet it should be noted that people from all walks of life may acquire one of these "pet names" along the way. They have, too...for literally thousands of years.

All About The Name-Changers

If the owners of pseudonyms had kept their original names, would they have achieved equal fame? Who knows? In the case of Walter Matuschanskayasky, whose father had been an Eastern Rite Catholic priest in Czarist Russia, it's debatable. This ordinary-looking but quick-witted fellow is known to Americans as Walter Matthau.

William Beedle, Jr., was a handsome, talented young man. But upon hearing his name, an executive of Paramount Studios exclaimed, "Beedle! It sounds like an insect."

The end result was William Holden.

Personalities who changed only one of their names aren't included in our pseudonym list that follows. For instance, Bing Crosby's given names were Harry Lillis; Gary Cooper was Frank; Chico, Groucho, and Harpo Marx were Leonard, Julius, and Adolph, respectively. Edgar Allan Poe was plain Edgar Poe until he added the name of the Virginia merchant who adopted him—John

Allan. Actor Rip Torn's last name was, surprisingly, Torn, but his first name was Elmore.

Interesting combinations crop up regularly. Some celebrities combined first names with last, switched their last names to first, or split their surnames into parts. Others "tinkered" only slightly: Gretchen Young became Loretta; Warren Beaty added a "t" to form Beatty; and Lorne Green rendered his surname more distinctive with a final "e."

For the most part, Hollywood directors, producers, and agents assumed the roles of "name changers" for their ambitious hired hands. The titles had to be easy to remember or, by contrast, unusual enough to make them distinctive and, thus, identifiable. It was customary for most actors, dancers, singers, and other entertainers to adopt these new names in hopes they would better reflect the purported glamour of their professions.

Another—and by no means the least important—consideration was: would the name fit on a theatre marquee and in advertisements? Would it convey the right "impression" to the multitudes? Would it alone imply strength, steadfastness, mystery, humor, warmth, or desirability?

Imagine, for a moment, a "fellow you can trust." He might well be called Gary Cooper...or Jimmy Stewart.

And Marilyn Monroe certainly stimulated a prettier mental picture than her real name—Norma Jean Baker—would have.

Or, "better keep an eye on this bird...he's sinister." Boris Karloff, no doubt? One wonders whether William Pratt—Karloff's given name—could have struck such terror in the hearts of movie fans.

Comedians got the message, too, for it's obvious the following lineup wouldn't have easily tickled the funny bones of an audience: Benjamin Kubelsky, Nathan Birnbaum, Stewart Konigsberg, and Joseph Levitch. A funny man should have a simple title, they must have decided as they changed their names to Jack Benny, George Burns, Woody Allen, and Jerry Lewis, respectively.

Likewise, Leonard Slye, Orton Hungerford, and Nathan Cox greatly enhanced their images as Western heroes when they became Roy Rogers, Ty Hardin, and Rod Cameron.

Noting what was happening right before their typewriters, Hollywood gossip columnists quickly joined the fray. In the time it takes to change a ribbon, Elda Furry became Hedda Hopper and Louella Oettinger emerged as Louella Parsons. Two sisters—Esther and Pauline Friedman—became Ann Landers and Abigail Van Buren, syndicated advisors to troubled readers of newspapers nationwide.

Serious writers have used pen names for centuries, often to preserve their anonymity or to differentiate a new book from a previous one (especially if the critics had frowned on the latter). Ellery Queen, the author of popular mystery fiction, is the signature name for the two attorneys who wrote the material: Manfred Lee and Frederic Dannay. Agatha Christie was Lady Mallowan. Female writers frequently chose masculine pseudonyms to improve their chances to be published—e.g., George Eliot and George Sand, who were actually Mary Ann Evans and Aurore Dudevant.

Politicians and statesmen, too, have been known to incorporate a name change or two. Josef Stalin discarded Dzhugashvili; Trotsky used the name of a former Siberian jailer to replace his given name, Lev Davidovich Bronstein.

Today, a multitude of requirements must be met in order to change a name legally. There are forms to fill out, fees to pay, identification and documentation to provide. But in any event, you're in highly celebrated company if you decide to do so!

Nicknames, Too, Have Met Fame And Fanfare

One of the first recorded—and widely recognized—nicknames was Plato, that of Aristocles the philosopher. So even the ancient Greeks were fond of tapping their favorites with pet names. But not all such diminutives have been flattering: consider how the English statesman, Richard Cromwell, felt when his countrymen, at one time judging him ineffectual, tagged him Queen Dick?

American presidents are by far our darlings upon which to bestow nicknames, particularly if their initials make dignified newspaper copy—i.e., FDR and JFK.

Even the infamous—including murderers—are granted nicknames for the purposes of the press. Jack the Ripper may never be forgotten. And because New York City killer David Berkowitz was dubbed Son of Sam, more people recall that ominous nickname than remember him.

Common sources of nicknames are a person's unique physical characteristic, skill, personality trait, or life circumstance. It was Beverly Sills' perpetually sunny disposition that earned her the pet name Bubbles. And is there any doubt why musician Thomas Waller was fondly referred to as Fats?

Not only are we fascinated with the art of selecting titles for our babies...we love naming them the "second time around" too!

Pseudonyms We Have Known

Kareem Abdul-Jabbar   Ferdinand Lewis Alcindor, Jr.

Edie Adams   Edith Enke

Nick Adams   Nick Adamschock

Eddie Albert   Eddie Albert Heimberger

Robert Alda   Alphonso D'Abruzzo

Woody Allen   Allen Stewart Konigsberg

June Allyson   Ella Geisman

Julie Andrews   Julie Wells

Ann-Margret   Ann-Margaret Olsson

Elizabeth Arden   Florence Graham

Eve Arden   Eunice Quedens

James Arness   James Aurness

Jean Arthur   Gladys Greene

Fred Astaire   Fred Austerlitz

Charles Atlas   Angelo Sicilioano

Frankie Avalon   Francis Avallone

Lauren Bacall   Betty Joan Perske

Anne Bancroft   Anne Italiano

John Barrymore John Blythe

Orson Bean Dallas Burrows

Barbara Bel Geddes Barbara Geddes Lewis

Tony Bennett Anthony Benedetto

Jack Benny Benjamin Kubelsky

Polly Bergen Nellie Paulina Burgin

Milton Berle Milton Berlinger

Irving Berlin Israel Baline

Sarah Bernhardt Sara Bernard

Joey Bishop Joseph Gottlieb

Robert Blake Michael Gubitosi

Claire Bloom Claire Blume

Nellie Bly Elizabeth Seaman

Shirley Booth Thelma Booth Ford

David Bowie David Jones

Fanny Brice Fanny Borach

Charles Bronson Charles Buchinski

Mel Brooks Melvyn Kaminsky

Yul Brynner Taidje Khan, Jr.

George Burns Nathan Birnbaum

Richard Burton Richard Jenkins

Red Buttons Aaron Chwatt

Michael Caine Maurice Micklewhite

Taylor Caldwell Janet Taylor Caldwell

Michael Callan Martin Caliniff

Dyan Cannon Samile Diane Friesen

Truman Capote Truman Persons

Al Capp Alfred Gerald Caplin

Kitty Carlisle Catherine Holzman

Diahann Carroll Carol Diahann Johnson

Lewis Carroll Charles Lutwidge Dodgson

Mama Cass Ellen Cohen

Igor Cassini Igot Loiewski

Cyd Charisse Tula Finklea

Chubby Checker Ernest Evans

Agatha Christie Lady Mollowan

Lee J. Cobb Lee Jacoby

Charles Coburn Colin McCallum

Nat King Cole   Nathaniel Adams Coles

Confucius   K'Ung Fu-Tzu

Sean Connery   Thomas Conner

Robert Conrad   Conrad Falk

Alice Cooper   Vince Furnier

Jackie Cooper   John Bigelow

Frank Costello   Francesco Castiglia

Lou Costello   Louis Francis Cristillo

Joan Crawford   Lucille Le Sueur

Tony Curtis   Bernard Schwartz

Bobby Darin   Walden Robert Cassotto

James Darren   James Ercolani

Doris Day   Doris Kappelhoff

Patrick Dennis   Edward Everett Tanner, III

Billy De Wolfe   William Jones

Phyllis Diller   Phyllis Driver

Troy Donahue   Merle Johnson

Kirk Douglas   Issur Danielovitch Demsky

Melvyn Douglas   Melvyn Hesselberg

Mike Douglas   Michael Delaney Dowd, Jr.

Bob Dylan   Robert Zimmerman

Barbara Eden   Barbara Huffman

George Eliot   Mary Ann Evans

Dale Evans   Frances Octavia Smith

Douglas Fairbanks   Douglas Elton Thomas Ulman

Alice Faye   Alice Leppert

W.C. Fields   William Claude Dukinfield

Rhonda Fleming   Marilyn Louis

Redd Foxx   James Elroy Sanford

Anthony Franciosa   Anthony Papaleo

Arlene Francis   Arline Kazanjian

Connie Francis   Concetta Franconera

Betty Furness   Betty Choate

Greta Garbo   Greta Gustafson

Judy Garland   Frances Gumm

James Garner   James Baumgarner

Mitzi Gaynor   Francesca Mitzi Von Gerber

Paulette Goddard   Marion Levy

Samuel Goldwyn   Samuel Gelbfisch

Elliott Gould   Elliot Goldstein

Cary Grant   Archibald Leach

Buddy Hackett   Leonard Hacker

Paul Harvey   Paul H. Aurandt

Helen Hayes   Helen Brown

Susan Hayward   Edythe Marriner

Rita Hayworth   Margarita Cansino

O. Henry   William Sidney Porter

William Holden   William Beedle, Jr.

Judy Holliday   Judith Tuvin

Rock Hudson   Roy Scherer

Engelbert Humperdinck   Arnold Dorsey

Evan Hunter   Evan Lombino

Kim Hunter   Janet Cole

Betty Hutton   Betty Thornburg

Dean Jagger   Dean Jeffries

Elton John   Reginald Dwight

Al Jolson   Asa Yoelson

Jennifer Jones   Phyllis Isley

Tom Jones   Thomas Jones Woodward

Boris Karloff   William Pratt

Veronica Lake   Constance Ockleman

Dorothy Lamour   Dorothy Kaumeyer

Ann Landers   Esther Friedman

Michael Landon   Michael Orowitz

Mario Lanza   Alfredo Cocozza

Carol Lawrence   Carol Laraia

Steve Lawrence   Sidney Leibowitz

Brenda Lee   Brenda Lee Tarpley

Gypsy Rose Lee   Rose Louise Hovick

Janet Leigh   Janette Morrison

Vivian Leigh   Vivian Hartley

Jerry Lewis   Joseph Levitch

Art Linkletter   Arthur Gordon Kelley

Carole Lombard   Jane Alice Peters

Sophia Loren   Sophia Scicoloni

Peter Lorre   Lazzlo Loewenstein

Diana Lynn   Dolores Loehr

Shirley Maclaine   Shirley Beaty

Makarios III   Michael Christodoulou Mouskos

Malcolm X   Malcolm Little

Karl Malden   Mladen Sekulovich

Jayne Mansfield   Vera Jane Palmer

Dean Martin   Dino Crocetti

Tony Martin   Alvin Morris

Mata Hari   Margareta Gertrude Zelle

Walter Matthau   Walter Matuschanskayasky

David Merrick   David Margulois

Ray Milland   Reginald Truscott-Jones

Ann Miller   Lucy Ann Collier

Marilyn Monroe   Norma Jean Baker

Rita Moreno   Rosita Alverio

Muhammad Ali   Cassius Marcellus Clay

Arthur Murray   Arthur Murray Teichman

Annie Oakley   Phoebe Annie Oakley Mozee

Betsy Palmer   Patricia Brumeck

Louella Parsons   Louella Oettinger

Roberta Peters   Roberta Peterman

Edith Piaf   Edith Gassion

Mary Pickford   Gladys Marie Smith

Paula Prentiss   Paula Ragusa

Ellery Queen   Manfred B. Lee and Frederic Dannay

Donna Reed   Donna Mullenger

Joan Rivers   Joan Molinsky

Harold Robbins   Harold Rubin

Sugar Ray Robinson   Walker Smith

Roy Rogers   Leonard Slye

Mickey Rooney   Joe Yule

Susan Saint James   Susan Miller

Jill St. John   Jill Oppenheim

Soupy Sales   Milton Hines

George Sand   Aurore Dudevant, nee Dupin

Omar Sharif   Michel Shalhouz

Artie Shaw   Arthur Jacob Arshawsky

Simone Signoret   Simone Kaminker

Beverly Sills   Belle Silverman

Phil Silvers   Philip Silversmith

Sonny   Salvatore Bono

Mickey Spillane   Frank Morrison

Robert Stack   Robert Modini

Joseph Stalin   Iosif Vissarionovich Dzhugashvili

Ringo Starr   Richard Starkey

Connie Stevens   Concetta Ingolia

Robert Taylor   Spangler Arlington Brugh

Danny Thomas   Amos Jacobs

Tiny Tim   Howard Khaury

Alice B. Toklas   Gertrude Stein

Arthur Treacher   Arthur Treacher Veary

Leon Trotsky   Lev Davidovich Bronstein

Sophie Tucker   Sophia Abuza

Mark Twain   Samuel Langhorne Clemens

Twiggy   Leslie Hornby

Roger Vadim   Roger Vadim Plemiannikow

Abigail Van Buren   Pauline Freidman

Mamie Van Doren   Joan Lucille Olander

Voltaire   Francois Marie Arouet

Nancy Walker   Anna Myrthle Swoyer

Mike Wallace   Myron Leon Wallik

John Wayne   Marion Morrison

Shelley Winters   Shirley Schrift

Stevie Wonder   Stephen Judkins

Natalie Wood   Natasha Gurdin

Jane Wyman   Sarah Jane Faulks

Gig Young   Byron Barr

Nicknames: Notorious And Otherwise

John Quincy Adams   Old Man Eloquent

Horatio Alger   Holy Horatio

Gracie Allen   Crazy Allen

Ethan Allen   Robin Hood of the Forest

Aristocles   Plato

Louis Armstrong   Satchmo

Clara Barton   Angel of the Battlefields

Phineus Taylor Barnum   Prince of Humbugs

William H. Bonney   Billy the Kid

General Omar Bradley   Doughboys' General

William Jennings Bryan   Silver Tongue

President James Buchanan   The Bachelor President

Martha Jane Canary   Calamity Jane

Eddie Cantor   Pop-Eyes

Al Capone   Scarface

Rick Cerone (baseball star)   Italian Stallion

Lon Chaney   Man of a Thousand Faces

John Chapman   Johnny Appleseed

Brigadier General Claire Chennault   The Fox

William Frederick Cody   Buffalo Bill

James Corbett (boxer)   Gentleman Jim

Richard Cromwell   Queen Dick

Bing Crosby   Mr. Music

René Descartes   Father of Modern Philosophy

President Dwight D. Eisenhower   Ike

Queen Elizabeth I   Good Queen Bess

Mark Fydrich (baseball star)   The Bird

Ella Fitzgerald   First Lady of Song

Charles Henry Fowler   Apostle of the South

Irving D. Hadley (baseball star)   Bump

Fred Hall (musician)   Tubby

Admiral William Halsey   Bull

Jean Harlow   Blonde Bombshell

President William H. Harrison   Old Tippecanoe

Franz Joseph Haydn   Papa Haydn

Coleman Hawkins (musician)   The Hawk

President Andrew Jackson   Old Hickory

Harry James   The Horn

Claudia Alta Taylor Johnson   Lady Bird Johnson

Earvin Johnson (basketball star)   Magic

President John Fitzgerald Kennedy   J.F.K.

William Ladd   Apostle of Peace

Mayor Fiorello LaGuardia   Little Flower

Dorothy Lamour   Sarongstress

President Abraham Lincoln   Honest Abe

Mary Todd Lincoln   The She-Wolf

Ray Meyer   The Coach

Edson Arantes Do Nascimento   Pele

Jacqueline Bouvier Onassis   Jackie O

President Ronald Reagan   Dutch

James Whitcomb Riley   Hoosier Poet

President Franklin Delano Roosevelt   F.D.R.

President Theodore Roosevelt   Bull Moose

George Herman Ruth   Babe Ruth

William Shakespeare   The Bard of All Time

Percy Bysshe Shelley   Mad Shelley

Beverly Sills   Bubbles Sills

Frank Sinatra   The Voice

Edward Teach   Blackbeard

President Harry S. Truman   Give 'em Hell Harry

Sophie Tucker   Last of the Red-Hot Mamas

Rudolph Valentino   The Sheik

Thomas Waller   Fats Waller

President George Washington   Father of Our Country

John Wayne   The Duke

Ehrich Weiss   Harry Houdini

Walter Winchell   Big Blab Wolf

Chapter 10

Birthstones And Flowers: What They Mean

The Greek culture is responsible for the fascinating folklore that brings us birth gems and flowers. Exotic mythology surrounds these symbols; the wearing of one's birthstone was actually believed by the ancient Greeks to guard health and bring love and success in life.

If you need a gift idea for a new baby, why not present the child a bouquet of his/her birth flowers, accompanied by a note explaining their significance (for the parents' benefit, of course)?

Here's the fun 'n fancy:

Month	Birthstone	Birth Flower
January	Garnet: symbol of constancy. The Greeks named this elegant fire-red jewel for the seeds of the pomegranate.	Carnation (especially red)
February	Amethyst: symbol of sincerity. This gem was said to be a favorite of both Cleopatra's and St. Valentine's.	Violet
March	Aquamarine: symbol of courage.	Jonquil
April	Diamond: symbol of love that stays young forever. The ancient Egyptians began the tradition of setting diamonds in their wedding rings.	Sweet Pea
May	Emerald: symbol of success. Even more than the diamond, this jewel has been a favorite of emperors and kings.	Lily of the Valley

June	Pearl: symbol of health.	Rose (especially white)
July	Ruby: symbol of safety. The Greeks believed "July children" wearing rubies could go anywhere and not meet harm.	Larkspur
August	Peridot: symbol of happiness.	Gladiolus
September	Sapphire: symbol of mental and moral well-being. Helen of Troy proudly displayed her beloved star sapphire.	Aster
October	Opal: symbol of hope.	Calendula
November	Topaz: symbol of fidelity. The Greeks believed "November babies" who wore the topaz would be graced with insight.	Chrysanthemum (especially yellow)
December	Turquoise: symbol of prosperity. The ancient Persians wore this stone as an amulet to protect them; Southwestern American Indians carried on this tradition.	Narcissus